THE AU

CW00969682

Born in 1903, Donald Hall was educated at ... e
where he read English. He started his career as an ... il
marriage and ill-health unwittingly combined in ... a
in the USA to care-take a farm. This in turn led to a lengthy sojourn in New .... .d
ultimately to the well-received publication in 1932 of his first travel book, *Enchanted Sands*.

His next travel book, *Romanian Furrow*, followed in 1933 and soon after, Hall wrote his first novel, *No Retreat*, based on his Romanian experiences. Two further novels, *Perilous Sanctuary* and *This Other Eden* completed his pre-war output; 15 years were to elapse before the publication of his next work, the epic poem *The Phoenix Flower*, in 1953.

Hall returned to novel writing with *The Seeming Truth* (1954), based on his time in the Foreign Office in the Second World War, and then revisited his original literary genre with *Eagle Argent*, a travel book based on the Abruzzi region of Italy. His last novel, *The Crowd is Silent*, set in wartime Romania, was published in 1961.

His final works were an autobiography, *Ring of Words* (1964), a study of The English Medieval Pilgrimage (1965) and another epic poem, *Journey into Morning* (1972).

Hall lived in Berkshire and North Wales. He died in 1984.

ROMANIAN FURROW

By D J Hall

◆

Bene Factum Publishing

Published in 2007 by Bene Factum Publishing Limited
PO Box 58122
London SW8 5WZ
Email: inquiries@bene-factum.co.uk
www.bene-factum.co.uk

ISBN 1-903071-12-7 (978-1-903071-12-0)
© Text the assignees of literary Estate of D J Hall.

A CIP catalogue record of this is available from the British Library

Typeset by 01:02 Design, London
Cover by Fielding Design, London
Printed in Great Britain by Cromwell Press, Wiltshire.

CONTENTS

◆

FOREWORD

◆

In the inter-war years, a posse of English writers descended on Romania, more often than not behind the wheel of a motor-car, most of them bent on either having tea with Queen Marie or taking photographs of wild-haired gypsies. A few of them spurned this mode of travel and set off on foot – Walter Starkie, the eccentric Irish Professor of Spanish and maestro of gypsy music ('*Raggle Taggle*'); Philip Thornton, the BBC folk music expert and broadcaster ('*Dead Puppets Dance*' and '*Ikons and Oxen*'); the young footloose Patrick Leigh Fermor ('*Between the Woods and the Water*'); and the adventurous Donald Hall, the acclaimed author of the recently published *Enchanted Sand: A New-Mexican Pilgrimage*. Hall alone went one step further; he donned peasant dress and went to live and work as a villager.

Starting off in a remote village to the north of Curtea d'Arges, Hall soon mastered the language and learnt the customs, dances and songs of his hospitable if somewhat perplexed peasant hosts. Before long, he joined them in their maize fields, stripping the cobs row by row in the harsh heat of summer. Witnessing a birth in the fields, several weddings, the paparuda rain-making festival, curățat (a party to celebrate the husking of the corn), a funeral and a pomana (feasting of the dead) and other village rituals, Hall's beautifully observed record captured a unique way of life that had existed more or less unchanged for centuries, 'the earth its centre, the core of its existence.' Unwittingly, Romanian Furrow turned out to be the ultimate trip down the memory lane of this peasant culture as post-war communism and materialism combined to undermine it.

I was fortunate enough to have read Romanian Furrow just after my first trip to rural Romania in 1998 and was able to use it as a benchmark during my many ensuing journeys around the countryside. Although much has changed since Hall's sojourn in 1932, much has also remained the same. Hall's 'thick white cotton trousers of no shape and white, collarless smock with short, full sleeves and belted at the waist' may have gone but the open-sided carts or căruțe drawn by either horse or oxen remain, as do the everyday tools of ploughs, hoes, scythes and sickles. Likewise, the ancient ceremonial cycle of marriage, birth and death continues in more or less its traditional form.

In summing up his experiences, Hall wrote: "In the happiness of these people lay their strength. Because in the West we have made a world which is hard on us if we are not continuously busy; we have made work a standard of morality and affect contempt for what we call idleness. Even in our leisure we must always be 'doing' something. These people had no such fetish; they worked to eat, no more. They were not lazy. It was only that they had not forgotten the meaning of composure. "Later on, he admits that 'laziness is comparative' as he trudges exhaustedly back from a day in the fields as I have done many times myself! Romanian country folk still retain that sense of composure, possessing a calmness that comes through confidence in the purpose of their existence. Consequently, they are gentle and friendly, hospitable to a fault and staunchly loyal.

With the accession of Romania to the EU in 2007 many fear for the future of the country's thousands of subsistence farmers. I suspect that the strength of the bond they have with the land will prevail over the lure of urban riches and that their precious and jealously guarded way of life will continue in much the same way as before. However, this time they will have a choice.

Alan Ogden
July 2007

ROMANIAN FURROW

◆

CHAPTER 1

THE GREAT RIVER

◆

As I was trundled across Belgium and down into Switzerland I had none of the exciting thoughts which should have accompanied me. I had been tired when I had started, and continental third-class seats are hard. When I went to sleep people came into the carriage and trampled on me.

It was not until the train had entered Austria and was smudging the line of the Wallam See that something happened which stirred me from my uncomfortable lethargy, making me forget that my bones were coming through the seat of my trousers.

I had been gazing half-consciously at two thin, grey peaks which streamed upwards from the far side of the clear, emerald lake. The day was intensely hot and the grey rocks and blue sky took on a little of each other's colour, so that they seemed hardly a part of the vividly contrasting lake and lower mountains. Suddenly from nowhere, almost as though a piece of the sky had miraculously taken shape, a silver tube hung between the peaks and slid across the blue like moulded mercury.

One moment there was only the dirty train rumbling through one of the loveliest valleys in Europe, the next there was this messenger from Olympus, the Graf Zeppelin. It was the more uncanny because it was silent for me who sat in a roaring train. Then the railway curved and curved and the messenger was gone, silently as it had come, leaving only an empty sky, grey peaks, and green water.

But I had forgotten my hard seat and began to think once more of where I might be going. I knew nothing about Eastern Europe as I had never travelled beyond Budapest. I was going first to Romania. That alone was certain. I had been given a letter of introduction to some one there who might put me on the track of what I was seeking. But that was perhaps only the beginning; I did not know. Anyway, I had been told so many fantastic stories about the difficulties I should be up against in a country which people in the West seemed to think was half-civilized that I had little hope that whatever I might wish to do in that corner of the world would be realized.

It was late at night when I arrived in Vienna, and I went straight to the boat that was to take me down the Danube. It was almost deserted, for most of the passengers would come on board early the next morning; neither were there boats loading or unloading to waken the sleepy quayside. For a little while I walked up and down the upper deck to loosen my stiffness. Then finding a dark corner I wrapped myself in my overcoat and lay down on a seat by the rail on the river side of the boat. It was cool there after the stifling train; the air was river-drowsy. The night sounds were soothing, only the wash of the swift-curling current against the sides of the steamer, an occasional, long-echoing shout across the water which faded and was swallowed by the darkness, and the rumbling undertone of the city. Soon I was asleep.

I was awakened by the sun and the noise of the arriving passengers. Already the far bank was crowded with bathers running in and out of the water. Then the boat swung round and was away.

All day we poured downward with the river. At first I was restless. I began to wonder how, after two days in a train, I was going to stand the inaction of three days on a river steamer. But gradually I became fascinated by the inevitable power of the river; that anything so huge could move so swiftly was almost frightening. There seemed nothing but the river. True, there were large towns at which we stopped for a few minutes. There was Bratislava, capital of Slovakia, with its ruined castle ruling from a hill and low hills behind covered with vineyards. There was Esztergom, with its cathedral, also on a little hill. But they were unimportant to the river. It was as though the towns required those hills to shout their existence. They were passed and sank till there was only the river, with low, shingle banks and dense, loosely jointed eucalyptus woods. Behind those woods were great plains, nations, and important people, but I could hardly believe it. Every now and then broad, shallow creeks flowed into the main stream, building low breakwaters, behind which lay long, still pools where bronzed nudes, men of the river, bathed or mended nets. Beside these were only the countless waterfowl.

But on the boat the men were neither slim nor bronze and the women were very fat. So that sitting on the baking deck and thinking of my objective I decided arrogantly and arbitrarily, because there was no one there to contradict me, that what we have lost by culture is integral consciousness of mind and body, and gained instead large stomachs, and brains overcharged with knowledge 90 per cent of which is useless. We unshipped a few at Nagymaros and passed on.

On the opposite bank stood Visegrad, the ruins of a castle which the kings of Hungary inhabited in the fifteenth century, and which was destroyed by the Turks in the seventeenth, now only a signpost by the river of blood. But the names of the towns and villages were mainly only names to me, labels for places where men through the centuries had dared to use this great, rampant god, fought over it, dyed it red, cast flowers on it to appease it, and still remained its slaves—all but the fishermen, the men of the river.

As the fire went out of the day the line of eucalyptus woods was broken up by the fields, untidily, so that you could not tell where fields began and woods ended. Cattle stood in still masses wallowing to their bellies in coolness behind the shingle bars. And with the passing of the sun came more colour as the air cleared. Ahead was a dove-grey village against sage-green hills rising to deep-forested slopes. Beige ducks and black ducks bobbed in jumbled patterns on the unruffled water; overhead flights of them swept fast and loosely. White geese were grouped on the foreshore below low, mud-grey cliffs crowned with tasselled maize. The Danube was blue at last.

As we rounded a wide bend I looked back once more and saw an orange ball low down behind black poplars, throwing into uncanny relief a grotesque crane standing alone in the path of the glare on a silvery beach. Then the light clouds lost their reflected colour: the sky, the earth, and the river were all blending. I thought that the magic moment of the last colour was past and that it was night. Then came the wonder of the plains. Colour, not light, insidiously returned. The river became of white gold, and from the west sprang arrows of pink which leaped across the pale sky and vanished, a very reflection of the sunrise underneath the world. In the east lay a bar of flame edged with green, and on the water was a still flame, and hanging in it was a boat black as Charon's ferry between the hills that looked like mountains.

Night had really come when we reached Budapest. Although the steamer waited there over an hour I felt no inclination to go ashore. The river had laid its hold on me; it was carrying me away; if I stepped ashore for a moment perhaps it would not wait for me. So I hung over the rail watching the lights flickering on the turbid water, listening to the grumbling of the town, the chatter of the people as they strolled under the acacias at the water's edge while music came and went in the summer's night. But that grumbling, that chatter and music came only from Pest. Across the river from Buda came few sounds. It lay there brooding, ancient, and dotard, with its royal castle on a hill winking one eye and hearing dimly the garrulous modernity of its child.

As the river took us again I lay down in my corner. Before I closed my eyes a black bar shut out the stars for a moment—a bridge. The bridge from which only thirteen years before Bela Kun had caused scores of his fellow-creatures to be thrown to the river during his one hundred and thirty-three days of Red Terror.

A chill breeze arose in the night and I did not sleep well. It was not yet dawn when I began to walk about the deck to warm myself. Just before the sun rose the wind dropped, and over the ever-broadening river, now thickly banked with eucalyptus woods, hung a pale stillness, a breathless waiting for the sun. Then, as it came, a grey crane slipped slowly upwards from a naked island over a pink river.

Hour after hour we were swept along. There were no hills, not a rise anywhere in the earth's surface. The river travelled southward now, and I wondered if there could be anything to the east between me and the Ural Mountains. Yet the monotony was impressive, bearing a dumb and tremendous strength.

A man came up to me and we talked. He was a Romanian Jew, an ardent Zionist. We had not been together five minutes before he launched into a history of the Jews, declaring that now at last they were coming into their own. I know lamentably little about the Zionist movement, so I listened with few interruptions.

"Why not should we have a place to call our own? Must we always wander?" he cried passionately. "For myself and my family I have bought ten acres of land in Palestine. Next year I go there to see it and make my plans. Later I will go to live there. Every year I send subscriptions to the Zionist societies, and my son has a little box in which he always puts small sums."

"But," I asked innocently, "are the Jews really returning in such large numbers as you say? I find it hard to believe."

"No, you do not believe. No one ever believes a Jew. I say that there are thousands from every country in the world returning to their land every year. They have built Tel Aviv, one of the loveliest cities in the world. The Government sold to the Jews a desert it knew not how to cultivate, thinking, 'Ah, the Jew will starve there.' But the Jew has worked and worked: now it is a paradise. I say to you that the world has still to see the greatness and the power of the Jews." He turned on me. "I love the English; they are a great people; in England I have many friends. But "- his face became suddenly twisted with fanatical rage - "as for those men, and for one man in particular, who stops us because of the Arabs, and stirs up always hatred against us, I would that he should hang always by the wrists till the mosquitoes have him - yes, have him piece by piece."

Feeling on dangerous ground I asked him to give me some proof of these charges.

"Proof !" he cried. "What proof do I need but the blood of my people murdered? You write. I will give you the chance to write the greatest book that has ever been written - great as the Bible. Go now to Palestine instead of wandering without purpose. I will give you introductions to all the most important Jews there. You can see and hear everything. Great as the Bible it will be, and the world will hear the truth about the Jews."

Then he left me wondering indeed if I should go to Palestine and write such a book. But that the world would hear my word I very much doubted. The man's fanaticism fascinated me, excited me so that that night on my bench I lay for long watching the stars and thinking insanely of this great project and the star that shone in the East. The next day I saw the Jew, but he was calmer. We did not meet again till I landed in Romania. His last words were, "I will ring you up to-morrow at your hotel. We will meet and I will give you much information. That book: it will be bigger than the Bible." And I never saw him again.

That night we came to Belgrad. I could not see how we approached it. The river seemed to have widened vastly; its course was untraceable and the lights of the shipping appeared to be a continuation of the stars. I felt we must be spilling over into space. The river was in fact half a mile wide, and the town being on a promontory washed on one side by the quarter-mile wide Save explained the mystery. But it was not till we came up to the massed lights of the town that any sense of reality came to the scene. For half an hour we stayed at the shabby quay while dark, barefooted men naked to the waist leaped around like monkeys unloading cargo. No sound came from them but inarticulate grunts. Then impassively they watched us go. Of the town I saw nothing but the lights, my memory of its history looking through them only at its fortress, the Roman Singidunum, which, ruined many times, became at length for centuries one of Europe's bulwarks against the Turks. A not very successful one, for the enemies of Eastern Europe occupied it, though thrown out at intervals, until 1867.

At four in the morning there was a gentle, scrunching sound, then a jerk, and the ship's engines quietened down. There had been no rain for weeks and the river was very low. We lay aground for some time while the dawn lightened and a smaller steamer came alongside to which the passengers were transferred.

Now on the left bank the hills of the Banat fell steeply to the water's edge. As we went onwards groups of peasants wearing bright costumes waved to us gaily, the early morning sun glancing from their scythes. That first glimpse of colour in the people thrilled me. Yugoslavia too on the right bank was becoming rugged. The river narrowed and the shallow water swirled and foamed. The hills rose to mountains. At last the great river seemed at the mercy of the land. Never for more than a few hundred yards did it run a straight course, but was squeezed and twisted first one way then the other. The jagged Babakai Rocks rose from the middle of the stream, the water thrashing round their base. Then came the rapids. But as if to give the struggling river a rest we came suddenly into a swift-flowing, lake-like basin. It was not for long, being only a prelude to the gorge of Kazan, where the river proved its strength by piercing the southern Carpathians. Here it was calmer; the river flowed swiftly three hundred feet deep between the walls of rock not two hundred yards apart. Ten feet above the river on the right bank a goatherd drove his flock along a winding ledge, at points where the rock fell perpendicularly to the water galleries carried the track. Over eighteen hundred years ago Trajan had built that track, and there had led his legions when he came to conquer Dacia: Dacia that could be occupied but never has been conquered. Romans, Goths, Huns, Scythians, Charlemagne, and finally the Magyars, all have subdued it for a time; it remains unconquered. At the end of the gorge in letters hardly legible is cut into the sheer cliff: Imp. Caesar Divi. Nervae F Nerva Traianus Aug. Germ. Pont. Maximus. . . . From the beginning of history and for all its length men have fought over this river.

Then again the banks fell back; we came to Orsova and found a larger steamer waiting to take us on. A mile below, a narrow, wooded island with a minaret white against the green split the stream; Ada-Kaleh, a Turkish outpost left behind in 1867 when the ever-pressing thorn in the side of Europe was being slowly withdrawn. Forgotten by treaties it did not cease to be Turkish until the Great War. None but Turks live there now; they wear the fez and live as their forefathers have always lived.

For the last time the river narrowed. Through the two miles of the rock-strewn Iron Gates the Danube poured, unnavigable but for a passage close to the right bank where the bed had been blasted to clear a way.

Then gently the mountains fell to hills, the hills rolled out and flattened away to the horizon, and I saw at last the great Danubian plain where the river flows more and more mightily to the Black Sea.

Away to the left stretched Oltenia, Romania. Looking at it I wondered if indeed I could ever wander alone through such a land. I seemed to have lost all sense of time and distance since I had been on the boat and felt that

I must have come to the far ends of the earth. Down by the water's edge were herds of swine which wallowed and scattered from the steamer's wash. Wells with long, horizontal beams balanced on forked uprights stretched their dark arms against the paling sky, the low cliffs were golden in the last light. Far back from the right bank in Bulgaria there were violet, Balkan mountains. The land below them looked like a fertile desert, making me think of New Mexico where I had not been alone, and nostalgia for my good companion, Henrietta, overcame me there in the stillness of coming night over the silent river.

But I was terribly hungry, and no one knew the time. Somewhere, I do not know where, we had changed from Middle to Eastern European time. There was divided opinion in the cook's galley. Until the matter was settled no one could get on with the cooking. At Vidin, a Bulgarian town, they had decided. But instead of eating I stayed on deck to watch the sunset touch the minarets and mosques, and later found some cheese and fruit I had forgotten in my rucksack.

It was my last night on the river. There were fewer passengers now, and most of them were sleeping down below. Here and there a figure lay huddled on the benches. But there was no movement, no sound anywhere as I walked up and down the deck or paused to watch the ghostly glimmer of the boat's wash. It was one of those rare moments when time ceases to exist, when there is nothing to tell you that you live in the twentieth or any other century. I might as well then have been floating on a raft at the birth of history or moving on the ice that will still that stream at last when the sun is dead and there is always night.

In the end I returned to myself. For what had I allowed this river to carry me away? In the morning I should be landing at Giurgiu, Romania, still with no idea of where I was going. I had been told that in Romania I should find alone in Europe a people who still lived close to the earth, whose whole philosophy was of the earth, who still thought as I did that the things which really mattered and had power were the earth, the sun warming it and the rain cooling it, the wind rustling the fields of corn, love in spring and birth in winter.

For those who must for ever be reasoning the whys and wherefores, who must always be reaching for the stars whether through the maze of intellectualism, religion, or in a scientifically conceived rocket-car, there can be no directness of apprehension. "There is nothing in the intellect except what was first in the senses. "They who have seen wild geese fly over frozen marsh-lands, who have gazed long at a square of clover on a furrowed down, and lain under the stars, all with no thought, but have only felt their beauty, alone have touched eternity.

In the morning, as we approached the shore, there were men driving great ox-carts along the river's bank. The long-drawn music of their voices came over the water and was borne away. I did not know then what they sang, but later when I heard the song again I learned the words:

On the banks of the Danube
Go the youths with oxen.
Before the oxen
Go with lovely flowers
The finest of the young men.
The sun cries to the flowers,
"Go, dear flowers, more swiftly
For the great Danube is coming."

And the flowers lament:

"If we wait for the waters we shall
be carried away,
For we have no brothers if we stay
Nor sisters to be sorry for us."

CHAPTER 2

THROUGH THE GATEWAY

◆

So I travelled to Bucharest in a carriage filled with peasants and a million chickens. The next day I set out with my letter of introduction. The Romanian to whom it was addressed received me courteously.

"But do you know how primitive our primitive villages can be? "he asked with a doubting smile.

I replied that I did not, but was anxious to find out. I realized then how ignorant I was. Perhaps it was foolish to try to enter into the lives of a strange, earthy people whose language I did not understand and who might never have seen an Englishman. But I dared not go back on myself. When the man saw I had made up my mind he began to talk, first guardedly then keenly, of what I should find. At the end he said:

"I think I know where you should go. I will give you a note to a man who will guide you to a village and leave you there. That is, of course," he said with another quick smile, "if it is really what you want."

I left him feeling that I had made a friend. Needless to say he had spoken in English, otherwise I should not have understood a word he said. Then I looked at the name on the note, Octavian Fotina, and the address; it meant nothing to me.

Out in the street it was over a hundred degrees in the shade. I soon discovered that Romanians wisely sleep in such a heat. After three days of trying to find the evasive Octavian Fotina I felt that sleep alone would save me from dematerializing. But sleep I could not. Though for many hours in the heat of the day I knew for a certainty that every one was dozing behind closed shutters there always seemed to be enough street noises to keep me angrily conscious. And at night the noise was shattering with the concatenation of the awakened city.

On the fourth day I discovered Octavian Fotina. He was a superb-looking creature over six feet in height and massively built. His skin was dark as an Indian's, his eyes brown and full of light, and when he smiled, which was often, a double row of silver teeth flashed under his black moustache. He wore a strange mixture of town and peasant dress-a white, embroidered shirt belted at the waist and hanging loose outside his white flannel trousers, a double-breasted black coat and a felt hat. Having read the note I handed him he began to talk rapidly in Romanian, which, but for a few words of French, was all the language he knew. When he realized my ignorance he slapped me heavily on the shoulder and laughed gargantually. Then laboriously, with my dictionary and the French words he was anxious to show off, we came to an understanding. He knew a village, and the next day we would start together if I could meet him early at the station.

That evening I went out to buy many films for my camera and call on an Englishman I had met in the town.

"Of course you're taking an automatic or something of the kind with you," he said.

I recalled a conversation I had had with an old Indian trader when I had first gone to New Mexico.

"I never carried a gun in my life," he had said. "Few bits of string and an old pipe is all I had when I was young, and the country was full of blue murder then. If a man's going to shoot you, he don't tell you about it first, so what's the use. An' if he knows you have gun, he'll be more careful about hittin' you first time. I've been threatened often enough, but threatened men live long."

I had followed his advice then; why not now?

My acquaintance shrugged his shoulders.

"Well, you know your own business. I wouldn't wander about the country without one. Don't say I haven't warned you."

I was on the station by half-past six the next morning, and found that the train would not leave till eight. I realized then that Octavian Fotina had not expected me to get up so early and so had given me plenty of margin. But I was new to the country and had not yet learned that time there was of practically no importance. So I walked about the platform thinking how pleasant it was to be again where clocks did not govern the movements of the inhabitants, but wishing I had known it earlier. Five minutes before the train was due to leave Octavian Fotina appeared, beaming with pleasure as at an unexpected meeting.

As the train left the outskirts of Bucharest and entered the vast corn plains I still had only the vaguest idea of my destination. Curtea de Argeş, my ticket said, I knew something of that town, and tried to place it on a map in my mind's eye, a little town near the foothills on the south side of the Carpathians about four hours north-west of Bucharest. But beyond that my imagination would not carry me.

We stopped at nearly every small station. Always the platforms were thronged with peasants selling grapes and peaches, and always Octavian Fotina leaned out of the window and bought great bunches of grapes, which he laid in my lap. I tried to explain to him that I could not possibly eat them all, but he showed me by example that I had no idea how to eat grapes. Tilting his head back he suspended a bunch over his gleaming mouth and then gently pressed it home. I had spent nearly all my spare moments in Bucharest trying to pick up the language from books I had brought with me. But though already I could understand a little I could speak almost nothing at all, so our conversation was hardly fluent. Seeing then that buying me fruit was the only way to entertain me, Octavian varied it by buying peaches. And I, thinking he must be wasting a fortune on me, bought him a bunch of grapes in return, and discovered that they cost about a halfpenny a pound. I could feel myself distending, and was wondering how long my stomach would hold out, when we arrived at Curtea de Argeş.

Even as we left the station and were walking through the narrow streets of the little town I was conscious of having stepped into a world of which I knew nothing. It was market day and the streets were filled with peasants from all the country round. Căruţe[1], heavy, open-sided carts piled with white cabbages and brilliant peppers, trundled lazily along the rough roadways. I had never imagined that the people's clothes could be so lovely. I had seen pictures of peasants in national costumes and had imagined that they had been specially posed. But here were men and women at whom I stared in wonder. The very roughest of the women wore blouses covered with exquisite embroidery in clear blues, reds, and yellows, and the men, their close-belted shirts loose over their thighs above tight, cotton trousers, wore embroidered sheepskin waistcoats.

The journey to Fotina's house was a long one, or so it seemed, for every few yards he stopped to talk with a friend, while I shifted my rucksack a little and waited in the grilling sun. At last on the outskirts of the town we came to it, white and square, set back in a little garden up a high flight of steps. Fotina led me to a trestle table in the shade where we sat while peasants came in, talked, and departed. It was drowsy and quiet there. The sun filtered through the acacias as I listened to the murmuring voices blending with the hum of the bees and watched the tired flowers in the little, dried-up garden droop their heads in the heat. Presently he turned to me and explained that as it was a fast day his wife and daughter would not eat with us, but soon they would bring us food. He rose to fetch a bottle of ţuica[2] a strong plum brandy. We drank and nibbled olives.

"Smarandica," he called, "the Englishman is ready for his dinner. And

---

[1]Pronounced Carootsay [2]Pronounced tsweeca

Anicuţa[1], where is she?"

They came with dishes, Smarandica, his wife, and Anicu-a, his daughter, one of the loveliest creatures I have ever seen, a soft colour on her dark, oval face, and bright, dancing eyes.

"She is clever, my *Anicuţa*. Aren't you, my bird?" He pinched her cheek and she wheeled away. "She is only eighteen. Presently I will show you her diploma. But now we will eat."

We ate, as only Romanians know how to eat, immensely and well. First mamaliga, a kind of solid, corn pudding, soup, a whole roast chicken, with a plate piled high with salad, and much wine. More and more peasants came in to talk. I ceased to try to pick out words. The warmwrapping air and the voices became hypnotic. Fotina took my arm and led me to the house.

"You must sleep; there is still some way to go."

On the right of the doorway was a little room filled with his best furniture and bric-à-brac. Photographs and holy pictures decorated the grotesquely papered walls. His wife and daughter followed us in and on a plush couch spread a clean white sheet. I looked at it in dismay and pointed to my riding-boots. But my protest was adamantly ignored. I lay down and was covered with another white sheet, the green shutters were closed, and I was left alone.

A cloak of isolation drew around me in that room, spotless and stuffy with disuse, and I tried to let my mind float upwards, to look down on my surroundings, and adjust itself. Through a chink in the shutters a spear of sunlight touched the floor, the voices outside became blurred and distant, an imprisoned fly buzzed and was silent. My eyelids drooped, but at a gentle sound they lifted lazily. An oval face with eyes bright with mischief peered around the door. "*Anicuţa*," whispered an outraged voice in the passage. There was a giggle and the door closed. I slept.

A knock on the door awakened me. The spear of sunlight had gone from the shutter. I jumped up and found Fotina outside.

"You have slept long. We must go. But first some *dulceaţa*[1] to refresh you."

His wife came up with a tray on which were little saucers of cherry jam and glasses of water. Outside a man was calling.

"Octavian, the automobile is here."

The air was cooler as Smarandica and *Anicuţa* laughingly waved us on our way. It was an event, a funny Englishman who did not want to sleep in his boots and was going to live with peasants. They hoped I should come back and tell them about my adventures. But I never saw them again;

though for a time I thought of brown *Anicuţa* and how beautiful she was, until I saw others as beautiful as she in that country of handsome men and lovely women.

The road, or rather furrowed track, wound gradually higher by little round hills. I sat in the back seat of the car squeezed between Fotina and a very fat man whose name I did not discover. They shouted to one another across me, trying to raise their voices above the crashing of the old car as it bounded over the pot-holes scattering clouds of dust and stones. We stopped on the curve of a hillside to mend a puncture, and I saw for the first time beyond the folding pattern of the foothills the high line of the Carpathians. Then we slid down again through birch woods to a farm. The owner, Pavlovici, welcomed us. We stayed an hour, beguiled with dulceaţa[1] and Turkish coffee, while Fotina talked endlessly. Even I could tell that he was repeating himself over and over again, but he liked the sound of his own voice. So did Pavlovici and my nameless companion; so do all Romanians. But why not when they have such a pleasant language and clocks are only ornaments?

As we set off again I felt as though the day could never end; behind me it stretched infinitely; the future had now become a blank. We stopped again at a village, and I thought that at last I had arrived. But no, after a few minutes we went on again. The sky was paling, and still we bounced on. At last when the trees were growing shadowy by the roadside we drew up at a little house set back from a village street. Fotina stepped out with a proprietary air.

"Here! This is where you will live."

I climbed wearily on to the road.

"Dumitrescu !" shouted Fotina. "Nicolaie Dumitrescu !"

A peasant came across the yard from the house.

"Yes, your honour."

A seemingly endless conversation ensued, in which I was the central figure under discussion. Then Fotina turned to me.

"This is Nicolaie Dumitrescu." I was not surprised. "You will stay with him as long as you like. He is a good man. Good-bye! I hope you will enjoy yourself."

Shaking my hand warmly he stepped back into the car and was gone.

The peasant stood there beaming. Then he took my hand and wrung it, speaking at such a speed as I had never heard any man speak before. But he was in no hurry to take me into his house. It was evening, every one had returned from the fields. Already he could see some of his friends coming down the road. In a few minutes I was surrounded by a crowd of

---

[1] Pronounced dulchatsa

them all anxious to make my acquaintance, all wishing to make me understand that they were pleased to see me. I wished I could have replied to their gracious reception; but even such words as I knew would not come from my tired brain, so I only smiled and tried to look intelligent.

Dumitrescu must have told his friends I was tired, for they politely withdrew as he led me through a gate across a yard to his house. It was dark now, and as I followed him up a four-step ladder I stumbled. But he took my hand and helped me on to the veranda into a little room, where he left me. In a moment he was back carrying a lamp and followed by his wife, two little girls, a baby, and his son aged about twenty. He introduced them to me in turn.

"My wife, Maria. These are Filofteia and Florea, and this" - he touched the baby - "is Dorina. My son Constantin will teach you Romanian. Sit down."

He pulled forward a wooden chair and I sat down. Constantin touched it.

"*Scaun*," he said.

I repeated the word mechanically.

"*Masã*," He touched the table.

Again I followed him.

"*Dicţionar?*" He tapped my pocket and I drew out my dictionary, which he eagerly examined.

"Good heavens," I thought suddenly, "are these good people going to try to teach me Romanian in a night?"

The day by this time had become so fantastic that no idea of protest entered my head. The lesson continued while the family stood watching. The little girls giggled, and every now and then had to rush out on to the veranda to laugh their fill. Some of Maria's friends came in and whispered in the doorway. I felt desperately hungry. Glancing surreptitiously at my watch I saw that it was ten o'clock. My thoughts must have been read, for when I looked again towards the door Maria had disappeared. After about half an hour she returned with mamaliga, an omelette and a plate of chillis. Setting them on the table she poked her husband and nodded towards the door. In a moment the whole family had said good night and I was alone.

I ate wolfishly and lit a cigarette, looking around the dimly lighted little room. It was whitewashed and hung with pieces of embroidered work, there were a table, two chairs, and a cupboard. I rose to examine the bed. It consisted of planks fastened to uprights at both ends. There was straw about an inch thick on it, over which was spread a blanket. Another blanket was folded to cover me.

Was any one coming back? I wanted to sleep. After waiting a little while I heard sounds from the next room as of people preparing for bed. No one came. Going out on to the veranda I saw a new moon rising over a haystack. "I hope it'll bring me luck," I thought. The night was silent; the sounds in the room behind me had ceased. A dog barked distantly and silence fell again.

CHAPTER 3

BIRTH IN THE FIELDS

◆

I AWOKE in the morning scratching. Looking at my body I thought that I must have caught measles. But it was only a flea. I captured him and his many relations quite easily. In Bucharest I had been told that I should be eaten alive in the country and I thought that this must be the beginning. In fact that night was the only occasion on which I was bitten, except by a dog, the whole time that I was in Romania. So easily was disposed of the first of the many horrid prophecies to which I had listened.

The morning was unexpectedly cold, but I welcomed its clearness. The air from the hills filled my room. Looking out I saw Maria milking a cow tied to the yard's fence. Presently Filofteia came in from the road, balancing on her small head an immense tub of water she had fetched from the village well. The day was alive with the noises of hens, ducks, and geese; piglets nosed snuffingly over the rubbish in the yard.

As I stepped out on to the veranda Maria called to me, asking if I had slept well.

"Yes, yes," I said and laughed. I said nothing to her about the fleas as I thought I might hurt her feelings or make her unduly solicitous. And I laughed because I really wanted to, became the air was so good and I felt so well. I had come to rest at last; I did not know where, I did not even know the name of the village. But I was content.

Maria cried to her husband that the Englishman was up and wanted water. He came grinning with a jug and emptied it over my head and hands as I leaned over the veranda. Then I ate a hunk of black bread and drank a bowlful of milk dipped from Maria's bucket while the sun rose up behind the walnut-tree across the village street.

So started that day and every other day in the village. Except that as I became more and more a member of the household the little girls, Filofteia and Florea, would burst into my room to tell me it was time to get up, often before the sun rose. And Constantin, or Costica as I called him when I came to know him better, would enter more ceremoniously to see me before he set off to teach carpentry at the village school.

Before I had met them I had feared that the peasants would be suspicious of me, would wonder what a stranger could want with them. Even a Romanian had told me in Bucharest that they might think that I was a Government agent sent to spy on them and that I must be careful. But from the first there was no sign of distrust. With the innate hospitality of their race they soon made me feel that I was one of them. Yet never before had an Englishman come to the village.

The language difficulty soon disappeared. Every time I opened my mouth I had to a find a Romanian word, so that it was not long before I could say ungrammatically what I wanted to and understand most of what was said to me. Wherever I went I was never without my dictionary, and Romanian talk French a great deal among themselves. Their own language is so simple, so essentially of the earth, which is their foundation and their life, that they cannot, using it, put nuances of expression into their conversation.

Of course the peasants wanted to know why I had come to their remote village. But when I told them, and I could not explain all, they understood. Among other things I wished to learn their customs and their songs.

"Songs, ah, yes, we will teach you many songs. But customs, obiceiuri . . ." They scratched their heads. What were their customs? That was a question not easy to answer right away. Where draw the line between old customs and everyday life? Since the memory of man it seemed their customs had not changed; they lived and died now as they and their earthy ancestors had always lived and died whether after a life's toil in the fields or fighting for their precious soil against Romans, Goths, Huns, Scythians, Turks, Magyars, or even Germans, as in the last war.

For the first few days I did little but laze about the village and its outskirts. The village lay all along the dusty valley road which later wound on and up through beech forests to cross the Carpathians. The little houses stood back from the road. Very few of them faced outwards, but were built with their doors and windows looking at the outbuildings across their spacious yards, as though they had turned one shoulder to the passing world, content with the completeness of their lives. Yet the most that passed down their road were bullock-carts or perhaps an automobile when a boyar came through from his country house. They were pretty too, those white houses with grey, wooden tiles; sometimes they were painted gaily with a red and blue frieze and had baskets of flowers hanging on the verandas. For every house, big or little, and few had more than two or three rooms, had foundations which rose high above the ground so that you went up steps to a pillared veranda from which doors led to the separate rooms. Pillared and with a carved rail, though the wood was often rotten and old the skilled craftsmanship still showed, and each man built his own house.

Where I lived we had only two rooms. Nicolaie Dumitrescu, his wife and children lived in one, I lived in the other. It seemed an unfair arrangement. Mine was the guest-room, and though my bed was only straw the whitewashed walls were gay with embroidered runners and little towels, woven and embroidered by Maria, pinned up in the shape of butterflies.

I never set out on my walks with any definite purpose, for I knew that I should be sure to meet some one anxious to talk to me, to show me his house or take me down the stream which had been diverted from the river to run the village mills. I do not know how many mills I saw in the first week. The stream raced between narrow banks and over it were built the mills, little square, wooden boxes perched on piles above a massive wheel. Sometimes they were for shredding out wool, sometimes for grinding corn. The flour-mills consisted only of two immense grindstones; the upper stone had a hole in its centre and a funnel was suspended above it filled with corn from which the seeds dropped. Beneath, a bin caught the coarse, golden flour as it poured from between the stones.

Tall willows stood by the stream and the water was dappled with sunlight. It was cool there. In the heat of the afternoon when the village slept I used to lie in the lush grass listening to the plash of the water as it poured under the mills, their wheels stilled. Sometimes a heavy ox-cart trundled lazily by me, so slowly as hardly to arouse the thick, white dust of the roadway, the driver dozing, his hat on his nose. The dull rumble and creak would sound long after the cart had disappeared, grow fainter till the warm silence came again with no bird singing.

Then, as the shadows moved beyond me and the peasants returned to their mills, I stretched myself and set off to see what I could find. So swiftly and insidiously the spirit of the people caught and bound me. There was no need for me to try to adjust myself to my surroundings. Perhaps I have a certain laziness of mind which when I am happy accepts without question.

In the happiness of these people lay their strength. Because in the West we have made a world which is hard on us if we are not continuously busy we have made work a standard of morality and affect contempt for what we call idleness. Even in our leisure we must always be "doing"something. These people had no such fetish; they worked to eat, no more. They were not lazy. It was only that they had not forgotten the meaning of composure.

One night when I had been in the village about ten days I was sitting in the yard of a house talking. Nicolaie Dumitrescu had taken me along to visit his brother-in-law, who made very good ţuica. It was airless and still. Men came in and squatted round the bowl into which we dipped our cups. The talk was slow and quiet. Some one had brought a lantern from the house so that I could look at the dictionary which fascinated them so much. There came a lull and I said:

"Nicolaie Dumitrescu, I want to work."

He scratched his head, looking puzzled.

"Work, domnule Englez, what kind of work?"

"In the fields, gathering corn, like you do."

"But you do not have to."

"I know," broke in his son; "he wishes to see how a peasant works. I understand."

"Yes, Nicolaie Dumitrescu," said another man, "to him it is strange. In England there are no peasants. The people live in towns. It is all over like Argeş, but much, much bigger, machinery everywhere and noise and smoke. I read once in Universul that -"

"But domnule Englez," interrupted Gheorghe Tamaş, a dark, big-shouldered man with a heavy moustache, "is it true that there are no peasants?" "No," I tried to explain, "there are peasants, but they do not live as you do. They do not own much land."

"But they are free? My father's father worked for the boyars and was very poor. He had to give his work."

"They are paid, Gheorghe Tamaş, and live in villages like this, only they have not much land." My Romanian was not yet up to long explanations.

He nodded.

"I think it is better here. We have no money at all. But we all have earth to grow our food. In Romania no one can starve. But the Government says we are lazy because we work only to eat and not to sell. We do not need much money. We should like more, but . . ."

Gheorghe Tamaş shrugged his shoulders and there was a general laugh.

The conversation drifted on, sometimes they addressed themselves to me, sometimes they just argued with one another while I sat trying to pick out their words. Ţuica always stimulated my faculties. It was as though this fermented plum-juice acted as an open dictionary, an interpreter of their language which had grown from the earth that nourished the fruit trees on their hillsides. So that the words and the fruit coming from one source mingled in my brain and spoke an understandable language.

What they said was true, though at the time I did not fully comprehend. It was only when I had been with them longer and had wandered to other villages, not only in the Old Kingdom but also in Transylvania across the Carpathians, that I realized their truth and the significance of their Government's action in giving the land to the peasants.

So I went into the fields and learned again that laziness is comparative. I soon discarded my clothes for those of the people, thick, white, cotton trousers of no shape and a white, collarless smock with short, full sleeves, belted at the waist and hanging loosely and easily over my thighs. One could toil in that with nothing beneath to prevent the air running softly over the body. No one, man or woman, wore anything beneath the outer garments. The dark hairs on the men's chests glistened with sweat, the curves of the women's breasts were drawn softly against their clinging blouses. Sometimes they too would draw themselves up and loosen their clothing to let a passing breeze play over their brown bodies. And at noon when the world slept they would free the cord at the side of their blouses' necks to suckle the babies that had lain in the shade while they worked. The unmarried ones, having no need to nurse, had their blouses fastened at the centre.

Steadily the men worked through the corn, row by row of six foot maize they stripped of their sheathed cobs. Behind us came the women, gathering the cobs from the baked earth where we had dropped them, filling flat baskets and bearing their great weight on their heads with lithe, easy carriage to the cart which stood in the corner of the field.

From dawn we worked on while the sun rose higher uncurtained in a deep blue sky. Ninety-five, a hundred in the shade. A haze quivered above the cracked earth, above the corn. The long leaves were beginning to droop, to crackle as we brushed them. Voices murmured always, sometimes rising together in slow, swinging song, a joke, a laugh, but never a pause, while the sweat poured from my body and my hands became bloody and blistered from my unaccustomed toil, tearing at the sheathed cobs.

Then with the sun at the meridian we ceased and moved to a clump of willows where a woman had made soup aromatic with many vegetables, and round cakes of mamaliga. We ate with our fingers, drank from our bowls, and afterwards were limp in the shade. A woman crooned over her child, men murmured gently and dozed. Then with the shadow gone we rose and went into the shimmering corn.

One day I was a little apart from the others, working a short row. I laboured mechanically, my mind detached yet also stirring only in a contented circle. This corn, this rough, dusty earth, the hills round and green with cool beech-trees: how good they all were. My body burned now to acceptance loved the fervent sun, drew in its strength till the very bones and entrails seemed to throb with some of its power. How altogether satisfying it was to feel that I was again a part of this good earth. Pull, drop, pull, drop, my hands were hardening, that was good too, what strength . . . the women would be coming soon to gather the uncircumcized cobs.

A cry and then a wail sounded behind me. I turned. The women were gathered in a knot some distance away bending over something. Three rows beyond me a man had stopped too, a look of puzzlement mingled with a little fear was on his face.

"Andrei Gheorghiu," I said, "what has happened? "

"I think it is Elena - Elena Brătianu. Her time had come."

He stood watching helplessly. I went over to him.

"But did she not know?"

"Yes, she knew. But she would not leave her work. Her husband said she was to -" He paused and crossed himself. "We are so near to death," he whispered.

"And new life," I answered, for I was frightened, thinking of the abundant earth on which I stood and the child that seemed over in that little group to be verily springing from it. The child was born, a son that was to inherit the earth. The women carried the mother to the willows and laid her in the shade. By the evening she held the babe closewrapped in her arms, crooning to it. The men went on with their work.

"It is a wonderful thing," said Andrei, when a woman called that all was well. "One moment we are not, the next we are." He scratched his head. "And in a little while again we are not. I do not understand. I think that only God knows. For it is the same with all things. Even with the crops; we sow the seed, but we do not know how it is made, we sow it and the sun and the rain make it grow till it bursts from the earth like that child was born. You have learning, can you tell me how? "

"No," I answered. "I do not understand either. But if we do not know that does not make life less good."

"It is not always good. I remember once . . . in a field like this . . ." He shook his head. "Only God knows."

Three days later Elena Brătianu was again in the fields, leaving at times her work to comfort the baby which lay in a blanket under the willows.

CHAPTER 4

THE DEATH OF ADONIS

◆

As the days passed till more than half the maize stood naked we seemed to be working harder, more swiftly. Perhaps I thought this only because the work came easier to me. But I mentioned it to Andrei.

"Yes," he said, "we work fast now because there must be rain soon."

"Why do you think that?" I asked, looking at the sky, which showed no signs of losing its cloudlessness.

"For three months we have had no rain, not since the beginning of June. Then we had the *Paparuda*, but it brought no rain. Now, when we do not want it, it will come. You will see. The *Paparuda* always brings rain at some time."

I asked him what was the *Paparuda*.

"When it is very dry and we have had no rain for a long time a gipsy girl dances through the village. She wears no clothes, only a few leaves and flowers. As she goes through the village the people throw water on her from the houses. All through the village she goes, singing and dancing, and others follow after her."

> *Paparuda-ruda*
> Come and drench us
> So that rain may come . . .

he sang and laughed. "It is a very old custom."

"*Paparuda*, does that mean anything like *paparoane?*"

"Yes, it is the same. But I do not know why it is called that."

Paparoane means a wild poppy. I was curious to know more, for the custom seemed a survival of sympathetic magic, that the effect resembles the cause, that if you want wet weather you must be wet. So let the *Paparuda* be drenched.

I asked Gheorghe and Nicolaie and several others about it, but they could tell me no more than that. The origins of customs that have been accepted for centuries are rarely known by those who have them. The fact that in a district of the Epirus the same custom is called περπερούνα, and a poppy essential to the dance, is no explanation though it might suggest a Greek origin. But when I heard later from Andrei of the festival of Calojan, which was clearly related to the ritual of Adonis, it made me think that the poppy had sprung from, or been stained by, the blood of Adonis even as the scarlet anemone was stained.

Winter has always been associated with death and spring with birth, especially by those whose whole lives are spent in watching the effect of the seasons on crops and vegetation. Religion personified this idea in a deity who annually died and rose again from the dead. For the Greeks it was Adonis, borrowed from the Tammuz of Babylonia, and for him they developed a myth distinct from that of the older god.

Zeus, called in to settle the struggle between Persephone and Aphrodite for the possession of Adonis, decreed that he should live for half the year with Persephone and half with Aphrodite. Ever since Adonis died on the tusks of a wild boar Aphrodite has mourned her love and will not be comforted. "Then he brought me to the door of the gate of the Lord's house which was towards the north; and, behold, there sat women weeping for Tammuz," said Ezekiel.

So the worshippers of Adonis saw in his departure to hell the fall of winter, and in his coming to the earth again the joy of spring. And with this resurrection of their god and the new life in nature was mingled also the older magical invocation of rain to aid their crops. For water formed an essential part of their celebration of his rebirth. The festival, whatever the peculiar rites in different parts of the earth, consisted always of days of sorrow and lamentation for the death of Adonis followed shortly by joy at his rebirth, symbolizing the rebirth of spring after the death of winter.

On the Monday before Ascension, Andrei told me, the girls of the village make an image of a youth which they place in a coffin and cover with flowers and aromatic plants. Then in the manner of a funeral they bear the coffin to the river's edge; one girl representing a priest, another a deacon, another carrying the funeral banner. With lamentations and tears they go, followed by a crowd of mourners, and bury the image beneath a tree by the river. After three days they go again to the place where they buried him. Singing sadly they unearth him:

> Calojan
> As our tears fall
> May the rain fall . . .

So singing, they take the figure and fling it into the river. This done their sorrow passes and they return joyfully to the village, dancing and crying that the youth has risen from the dead. So on the third day do Christians rejoice.

But it is more than an invocation for rain. Sometimes the girls sing:

> Calojan,
> Your mother has sought you
> Through the deep forests
> With burning heart,
> Through the open forests
> With suffering heart.
> Calogan,
> Your mother weeps for you
> With tears of blood.

That song of the bereft mother symbolizes the mourning of all women for their lost love, the beauty of which can never be recaptured but in rebirth. It is the oldest song in the world, the cry for love, for life, for fertility and increase. So interwoven are all the ancient myths and rites that only one object stands out through the dark haze that hangs over them, the desire for fertility. That is the primary desire of every man and woman, to have increase.

The feast of St. John the Baptist has taken the place of the pagan festival of water. In Russia the equivalent of the Calojan is celebrated at midsummer with similar rites. The name Calojan may have crept into the place of some earlier pagan name, Jan representing St. John, in the way that Christianity has elsewhere become inextricably mingled with the ancient religions whose thunder it has stolen.

It was so easy to understand, when talking with Andrei and the other peasants, why these old festivals were still important to them. The Orthodox Church filled with pageantry and colour, icons and gorgeous vestments though temporarily impressive was beyond their understanding. They were too simple for it to penetrate to their lives bound close to the earth. For them there was more glory in the sun than in lighted candles, more goodness in the smell of earth after rain than in swinging incense-burners.

Living with these people of the earth, these men and women who grew up like the corn, I began too to understand why Christianity had passed so easily from the vast peasant people of Russia. True, the Church there was ignorant and corrupt which it is not in Romania, but it fell largely because there was a lack of any real feeling in the peasants for their religion. They were overawed, sometimes loved to fanatical frenzy by the spectacle of the Church and the miraculous stories connected with it, these pleased their simple minds. But none of this ever touched their humble view of life, it was something beyond them which they made no endeavour to understand. Their ancient, pagan superstitions though were something they could understand; they were rooted with deep meaning for them, exercising a powerful sway. They have not lost these. The crosses of a superficial Faith can easily be swept away, but to uproot that which is of the essence of life itself requires a deeper probe and a wider understanding than the scientific Soviet possesses.

Peasants are not spiritual creatures. Andrei and my other friends might observe the formalities of the Church, but their wants were practical. They did not hanker after spiritual perfection. They were not irreligious, they felt the significance of the Church's ritual in an inexplicable way. But the myths linking the old gods with the sun and rain which caused their crops to grow and give them life were deep-stirring, potent. Dust they are, to dust they will return. But while they live the blood runs in them and there is passion, labour in women and in the earth, fear and laughter.

Andrei's fears were not fully justified. One night I awoke to the patter of rain. But in the morning the sky was clear once more with only a lightness in the air and the laid dust in the road to tell that there had been a shower:

"*Paparuda?*"

Andrei laughed.

"Surely. But she is too late. Now she has seen that, she will not come again. She only came to look."

CHAPTER 5

FISH-STALKING

◆

The great heat returned, strengthened it seemed by its day of rest after the rain. "It is strange," said the peasants, shaking the sweat from their faces. "Many years have gone since the summer was so long. See how the storks gather together in the fields. Now it is like July."

Each evening I found relief in the river which flowed near the village. It was shallow and turbulent, tearing over its stony bed, but so translucent that the sun's rays picked out the pebbles making them glow dully beneath the surface. It was mountain cold too, springing from the Carpathians. After so long a drought the water was low, tracing a winding course through the broad bed, most of which was dry and white, scattered with boulders brought down by the spring floods. Tall willows fringed its banks, silvery, unearthly beside the beech-trees which covered the hills rising beyond. Never have I seen such gentle hills. . . They rose up and folded one into another; thick with the soft green of their trees it was hard to tell where one ended and another began. They seemed to go on for ever.

Costica, the son of the house, went nearly always with me for these evening bathes. Lazily we strolled down the dusty road feeling already the coolness in store. Then off to the left down a little lane which lost itself in plum orchards. There was a steep slope down which we slid to a narrow, green field. Beyond, across the dry shingle, was a pool Costica knew, with a strip of sand by it and a tree that dipped its branches. As the wavelets tumbled against the branches they splashed the leaves with a fine spray; on the hottest day they always glistened freshly.

There we stripped naked, leaped and shouted in the tingling water. Lying on the sand we let the sun draw the moisture from our cooled bodies. And as we lay there Costica sang, looking up at the sky, slow songs that held in their music all the vastness of that land which travels over the hills to the plains of Moldavia, on, on to the Russian steppes behind the Dniester:

Green leaves, thick grass,

Rich river grass.
There is nowhere more lovely
Than our village.

Spring ploughs the hill,
Ploughs with two oxen.
How sweet is the cuckoo's singing,
On the bough by the water.

The music had a queer twist in it that caught at the heart. I would listen to the first two lines, hearing the long cry to the earth. There came a break in the voice, a sudden turn from slow contemplation to realization, "How sweet is the cuckoo's singing," and with that the music became quick with a lilt of joy, only to die away in an endless throbbing note that sang on in my consciousness long after the sound of it had passed.

I asked Costica why the songs had such sad music.

"They are not sad. It is only that when we sing we are thinking of the words. You cannot sing quickly and think. In the dances you hear gay music, for then we forget and only dance."

"Perhaps, Costica, it is also because your country is so big."

I had always this feeling about Romania, for although it is in itself not large it is a part of the great, geographical scheme which embraces southern Russia.

"Maybe. I do not know. But always we have worked the land, and such work is slow and hard. Also the winter and summer are very long. The spring is short and beautiful; the flowers do not last long; it is sad."

Often as we stood naked by the water's edge, women came by driving the cattle home from the fields. Sometimes they bathed near us, naked as we were, splashing and singing to one another. From the first I felt no embarrassment; they were not shy of their bodies or of mine.

One morning as I was setting out for the fields Costica came into my room carrying a gun. It was an immense old Männlicher and I asked him what he was going to do with it.

"This evening we are going to fish," he said.

"What, with that gun?" I asked incredulously.

"Surely; with what else?"

At which we both laughed, he at my surprise, I thinking he was joking.

"You will see," he said. "To-night we shall have fish for supper."

"I shall believe that when I see them on the table."

He went out laughing.

In the evening we set off through the plum orchards, Costica with his gun, I carrying a handful of cartridges out of which he had taken the bullets, stuffed them full of gunpowder, and put back the bullets loosely. I hoped that the gun would not explode.

As we neared the river bank the fever of the chase caught Costica; silently he motioned me to fall behind him. On tiptoe we moved to the edge, bending low. If we had shouted at the top of our voices it would have made no difference, for the stream was singing its loudest as it thrashed over the stones. But we were hunters seeking a difficult quarry. At the pool formed by a curve in the bank we slowly raised our heads and peered into the water. It was filled with tiny fish.

"Minnows !" I exclaimed.

"Hush ! They will hear you. There, they have gone already. You see, you must be silent. Fish have sharp ears."

Costica stood up, crestfallen at their escape.

"Now we will have to drive them down to the pool again."

"But they are very small."

Costica was a great joker. He knew it was absurd, but the chase enthralled him.

"Perhaps; but they are good to eat. Oh, very beautiful. Now ! Follow me."

Again we crept silently along the bank.

"There ! There they are. Now we will drive them."

We threw stones and sticks into the water while the fish scatted downstream. After waiting a few minutes we went back to the pool. There were the innocent little fishes swimming round in circles.

"Now," whispered Costica, "you must go into the water below them. When I fire, watch for the fishes and catch them."

I stripped and wading into the shallows waited expectantly. Costica slipped a cartridge into the rifle, lay down on his stomach and with the muzzle within an inch of the water pulled the trigger. Nothing happened.

"Dumnezeu ! "he muttered. "The powder is damp."

I was now taking the affair very seriously and could hardly bear the disappointment. Going ashore I condoled with him. He emptied out the powder and put the cartridge in his pocket.

"We will try another. Here is a special one I have filled."

I returned to my watch in the water while Costica lay down once more. This time there was a shattering explosion and fountains of water shot into the air. Costica danced on the bank.

"There they go. Quick, quick before the river takes them !"

I leaped about snatching at the stunned, silver bodies as they were turned and swept down to me by the current, throwing them on to the shore as I caught them. Costica counted.

"Twelve. That is not so bad."

"No," I said, standing over the glistening fishes not one of which was more than five or six inches long and slim at that. "But we shall need more for a good supper."

"Surely. We will go on down the river."

So we worked the pools, scrambling over the rocks and debris of the spring floods. At last when the sun had almost gone and we had caught about thirty I said it was enough. But Costica was fired with success, he wanted more, always more. We had come to a place where the stream ran close under high banks; Costica could see large fish there. But I could not catch them because the water was too deep. He went over to a little house among the willows and returned with a man carrying a widespread net on the end of a stick.

I did not offer to help. I felt lazy now and lay watching them. Behind me the wooded hills had fallen back beyond a field of close-cropped grass; across the stream the bank's face was ochre. All things stood calm and still in the late evening light. I turned on my back and watched the paling sky in which tiny, flickering points of light were beginning to appear. The mingled jingle and low resonance of cowbells drew nearer. The woman driving them before her stopped by me.

"What will you do if the jandarm finds you catching fish with a gun?"

"I do not know," I laughed. "I have not a gun."

"But Costica has, the bad boy. You will both go to prison, domnule Englez."

Her dark eyes danced. She was beautiful, her skin dark from the sun, only her small hands were roughened with toil. "It is fine here, is it not?

To-night there will be a moon."

She moved on, smiling mischievously.

"Good night," I said, laughing, "and thank you for your advice."

"Aie, aie," she cried to her cows. Turning on my stomach I called to Costica, still busy on the far bank of the darkening river.

"It is time to go home. I am hungry."

"I too. The fish are going to bed. I cannot catch them."

We were far beyond the village, and, as we went through the fields of corn, the moon rose over the hills.

> Give me your hands to kiss,
> For I die of quivering.
> If you go, I who stay
> Will be lonely in this great world,

sang handsome Costica, for the beauty of the evening went quickly to his heart. Quickly moved are he and his people. They love much, plunge deep and rise high who live close to the earth, know well its sorrow and its joy. The spring is short, the long summer full of passion, and in winter life is hard.

> Give me your hands to kiss,
> Let me with foolish suffering
> Weep on your soft breasts
> Beneath the rays of the moon.

CHAPTER 6

THE WEDDING OF ILIE AND ILINCA

◆

On a Saturday night when I had finished my supper I was trying to translate some songs which Costica had written out for me. The light was feeble and I had to sit with the paper close under the lamp. The words looked so much more melodious in their own language than in my translation that I had almost given up the task and was reading them aloud as Costica had written them, letting the slurred vowels and gentle cadence of their lines sink through my consciousness till I felt rather than knew their meaning. "Frunze de castan" was so much more liquid than "chestnut-leaves." I felt that the peasant poet was thinking then of autumn when the leaves were burned rich and ruddy, and that autumn was a prelude to a long sleep that seemed like death. Easy-flowing were those words as the seasons close with one another while the men watch the earth and sky.

The door opened and Costica came in with a bowl of water.

"What is that for?" I asked.

"It is long since I have shaved," he answered, "and to-morrow there is a wedding at Mora-tio."

I stroked by whiskery face.

"That is a good idea. I have not shaved for two weeks."

"Then we will both shave now. And to-morrow you will come with me to the wedding."

Finding a tube of shaving cream in my rucksack I offered it to Costica, but he eyed it doubtfully and said he preferred his own soap which was like a piece of brick. At the end we felt our smooth faces and congratulated each other on our appearance.

Already I had come once more to know Sunday as a day of rest. There was no creaking of bullock-carts and shouts of men going to the fields. When I lay down on the straw on a Saturday night I knew that I should sleep late the following morning. The habit had grown quickly. So when I awoke the next day the sun was already patterning the floor. But outside there was a sound of blowing and splashing of water. I jumped up and went to the door. Costica was in the yard stripped to the waist sousing himself.

"Good morning," he shouted. "Come and empty this jug over my head, and I will do the same for you. We must start soon, for the wedding begins early."

When we had washed we dressed gaily. Costica lent me a clean shirt with more embroidery on it than the one I had.

"Every one will be very smart," he said.

About nine o'clock we set off, Maria bidding us good-bye with appraising eyes. What a morning for a wedding ! The sky was cloudless, the air as yet was fresh with the promise of summer's ending. We crossed the river, balancing on a log thrown across the stream, the water glancing brilliantly and dancing over the stones. Beyond we entered the hills where I had not been before. At first we hurried along, clambering up the rough sheep-tracks, wending our way through the beech woods where the birds sang. Only at midday would they be silent. We sang too as we climbed the steep slopes and ran down into the little valleys, calling to one another to hurry. But as the sun rose higher our steps slowed. There was really no hurry after all, the wedding would last all day, and all night too, even perhaps into the next day. In a glade we sat down to rest, panting and wiping the sweat from our faces.

"This will not be a very great wedding," said Costica. "The bride and bridegroom have not much money. Perhaps we will have to pay our share of the feast."

"How much will that be?" I asked, looking up at the sky and lazily running the soft earth through my fingers.

"About twenty lei, perhaps. Not much."

It certainly was not much; the equivalent of ninepence. I wondered what kind of a feast it could be for that.

"And will there be many people there?"

"Surely; from all the villages round."

We set off again. At a hill-top I paused to look over the countryside. It was like the sea, like smooth, ocean rollers. But still, as though a hand had been held over the waters and a voice bidden them to become dry land. They were so little, those hills, and yet they seemed to roll for ever. Only to the north there was a high wall where the Carpathians stood mistily, their grey peaks almost blending with the sky. Entering a deep wood we crossed a stream where women were bathing their feet.

"We are near to the wedding now," said Costica. He jerked his thumb over his shoulder. "They are putting on their shoes."

The women of this country go always barefoot. Only at festivities or if they go into a town do they wear shoes. But the unaccustomed leather pinches their feet. So they wisely carry their shoes until the last moment. As we went on we passed more and more groups of women putting the last touches to their toilets.

The path now was well worn, before us at the top of a hill was a wicket gate. As we passed through it I halted and caught my breath. In a plum orchard stretching over an easy slope were hundreds of men and women, dancing, chattering, strolling, laughing. The sound of music came from among the trees. For a moment I thought, "If only it were blossom time." Then I knew that I was wrong, for the brilliance of the white flowers would have been too much in that orchard filled with the beauty of bedecked men and women.

The clothes of the women dazzled me so, that looking from one to another to find which one pleased me most I became confused. There were blouses with smocked necks, delicately embroidered in flower patterns; some were heavy with gold and silver thread, the full sleeves swinging with the weight; others were caught in at the wrist with widespread frills. Their white petticoats were concealed by thick, black aprons covered with elaborate designs in red, blue, yellow, violet, and green. The front aprons were the most elaborate, the patterns, whether geometrical or floral, were broadly designed interwoven with shining silver threads. There was never a mistake in the colour combinations, yet no design was like another. The infinite inventiveness and instinctive good taste of the women there attained perfection.

How gracefully too they moved ! To see them there in all their exquisite finery, gliding among the trees, it was hard to believe that in the weekday they worked and sweated like men. For they were so dainty, their little hands and feet looked more suited to the salon than the fields. Only when you have been with them and know how much they can accomplish, have seen the firm strength of those women, can you believe it possible. In their features too is none of the coarseness natural to the peasants of other lands; their beauty has a fineness in it which is strange and breath-taking to those who do not know the country.

Only the married women and the widows wore head-dresses. These were of all colours in silk or soft linen folded in a score of different ways, knotted at the nape of the neck and falling down the back. The older women wore them tied beneath the chin. There was an air of distinction in these head-dresses, almost of nobility. On Trajan's column there are carved such women. The unmarried girls had flowers in their hair.

Costica knew every one. As we went through the orchard we stopped to talk and joke with the men; Costica with a sly aside to the girls would set them blushing and giggling. Presently we came to a long table. It was formed of rough planks laid on sawn logs and only about a foot high, though nearly two hundred feet in length. At it were seated on logs a crowd of women feasting happily and well while the fiddler played around the table. Yet it was early, only eleven o'clock.

"Is the wedding feast started already? "I asked.

"Yes. But it will be better later. When these have finished we shall begin. The marriage in the church is not till two."

A man came up to us; he had an air of proprietorship about him. A carnation hung over one ear, and the white leather waistcoat over his flowered shirt was gaily embroidered.

"Come with me, Costica, to my sister's house. We will drink to her health - and every one else's," he added, laughing. "*Domnul Englez* too, of course." He slapped me on the shoulder, for he was feeling extremely happy.

So we went to the bride's house, a little two-roomed, whitewashed place in the corner of the orchard where for twenty years she had lived with her mother and father and brother. Its veranda overhung the hill, the ground fell steeply there, so that every evening the sunset must have set its flame on the white wall. The topmost branches of the tallest trees could not obscure the sky. Only when the sun had sunk below the farthest hills would that house be dark.

In the best room there were already three men friends of the bride's father sitting on the raised boards that served as beds at night. We joined them, and a woman brought in ewes' cheese, olives, and -uica. It was not long before there was a cry that the bride was coming. As she came in we jumped up and went into the next room, where, crowding round the doorway, we watched her being prepared for the wedding feast.

She was very young and fairer than most of her people. As the bridesmaids fussed around she sat with head lowered, only lifting her eyes nervously at times to glance at herself in the mirror held before her. Her hair was combed and brushed and decked with gold thread and a tiara of pearl beads. All the while the musicians, who had followed her into the room, played slow, melancholy tunes. I asked Costica what it was they played.

"I do not know all the words, but they are sad, so sad that they cannot sing them, but only play. It is because it is Ilinca's last day in her father's house. To-day she will leave it. Afterwards, when she returns, it will be only as a guest."

So they played on, with their lute and violin, their tambourine so sadly beaten, and the long, lingering notes tapped out on the ţimbală[1] hung around the neck of one of the players. I wondered then if Ilinca felt as affected as she looked, if she was thinking of her childhood, of the sunset flaming on the wall of her house on a hill, or if the longing for her waiting lover rose above all these sentimental thoughts.

For her lover was waiting, waiting on horseback by the door with his best man. Presently the best man began to shout a long speech. He was a superb creature with a broad, ruddy face and a crisp, black moustache, swaying on his horse as he spoke and refreshing himself from a large, painted plosca of ţuica. He was very fluent and very comic, for he had reached the state when all the world was his friend. The guests applauded his sallies loudly. As he finished, the bride ran out of the house with a tub. She splashed the water to the four winds and a good deal over the best man, and then ran in again. I never discovered the origin of this custom, but it signified good luck.

The bride was ready now and led the way to the table set among the trees. We sat down a hundred and fifty strong to the wedding feast. The bridegroom too was very young, a dark, slim, well-featured man. But they were both too nervous to eat all the good things on which we feasted. They just nibbled olives and drank a little ţuica now and again. I sat only two places from them and could hear all that went on. If the bride moved at all a bridesmaid would jump up with:

"There, Ilinca, you have disturbed your head-dress now," and would start fiddling with her hair, while poor Ilie, the bridegroom, would glance anxiously around and pat her hand, hoping that no one would notice the endearment. But of course some one was watching and then it was:

"Ha, Ilinca, he loves you after all. He will not be a bad husband. He will do more than pat your hand presently."

All the time the musicians played around the table. There was hardly a break between the songs. In every village there are gipsies who make the music for the people, swarthy rascals with music dancing in their blood, who can make their instruments say everything that is in the heart of men, the birds, and of the very earth itself. But at weddings the songs are nearly always comic. The leader with the violin draws his bow across the strings in a long note at the beginning of each song, singing the note at the same time to give it to the others.

> As I take the road, the world asks me
> Why am I so dark and thin.
> Anicuţa, little dear one,

---

[1]Pronounced tsimbaler.

I am thin for love of thee,
But dark-souled by no means,
Anicuţa, little dear one.

The wedding feast lasted nearly two hours. Soup, beef, chicken, peppers, and the dish that is always served at weddings, *piftie*, a not very appetizing mess of beef in jelly. It was all prepared in huge, earthenware pots by women in the orchard, cooked over wood fires, the scent rising with the wood smoke There were no implements, for, since there were not enough to go round, it would have been unfair to give them to some and leave others without them. So we ate with our fingers and drank from our bowls. The whole was washed down with *ţuica*. Washed down, that is, by my friends, *ţuica* was too strong for me to do such a thing. Yet no one became drunk. True, the hilarity of the party increased tumultuously, but every one behaved himself perfectly.

The bride's father came round with a hat to collect our twenty lei, while I marvelled that I had come to a land so rich with the fruits of the earth that I could eat and drink myself to a standstill for ninepence. And all the time Ilinca and Ilie sat solemnly at the end of the table, whispering to one another and hoping it would end soon.

Away through the trees those who had feasted earlier danced in the sunshine that filtered through the thick green of the orchard. Their spangles glittered, their clothes shone brightly, and their laughter mingled with the music as it went round and round the table.

The monk from the old monastery
One day there has entertained me,
And says to me, "Every one cries
Always of love, only of love.

Why then do I love God?
For what do I torture myself
If never in the world I love,
And cannot love a maiden?"

Then up we rose and danced too, The *Hora*, a circular dance with our hands on each other's shoulders, shuffling and side-stepping with the musicians in the centre. The bride's father carried the branch of a fir-tree, decorated with tinsel, a symbol of good luck.

The dance broke up and we went again to the bride's house. Crowding into the best room, those of us who could sat on the beds while the rest stood in the doorway or peered in at the window. In the middle of the little room Ilinca and Ilie stood while the best man made a solemn speech. Then kneeling before the bride's father and mother they received their blessing and admonition, after which every one assembled drank a glass of wine in confirmation.

Outside stood a farm-cart, its floor filled with clean straw, with a seat placed across it. The bride and her attendants climbed in. But before they set off bread was broken and salt scattered on the bride's head, an invocation to the gods that she should never want. Then off went the cart drawn by six white oxen up the dusty lane, the trees meeting overhead, the patterns of the sunlight making a lovelier carpet than any scattered rose-leaves. Ahead galloped Ilie, anxious to get to the church first to welcome his bride.

The church was set on a hill in a grove of beeches. It was very old, so old that no one could tell me its age. Century after century it had stood there blessing the baptisms and the weddings, bidding farewell to the dead, watching those people who rose from the earth, laboured all their lives on it and in the end returned to it, the warm soil covering the hearts of those who loved it.

It was so small that only a score of us could get into the apse, screened from the square body of the church, which itself could not hold, tight-jammed, more than thirty. As in all Greek Orthodox churches the altar was hidden. But in the centre of the apse was a table, the Tetrapod, on which stood two crowns, two glasses, and a loaf of bread. The priest had a fine-drawn, ascetic face; but for his square, black beard, he might have been a woman so delicate were his features. He read the service in a deep, sonorous voice. Taking Ilinca's hand he joined it with Ilie's, then taking the crowns, which were bands of bright metal, he placed them on their heads. Though they are only peasants they are crowned like royalty, lords in their own right of the soil.

Then the crowns were removed and a white ribbon was bound around their bodies fastening them together. The priest gave them bread and apple syrup from the two glasses.

While the ribbon was being untied by Ilinca's attendants the priest began to sing slowly the Tropar, "Isaiah dances before the Lord. . . ." The voices took it up, the singing became quicker. Stepping forward the priest took the bride's hand, a hand clasped mine, every one joined hands and danced. At first slowly, then quicker and quicker we danced around the table. It was not a solemn affair as I saw later in more sophisticated churches, but a gay, abandoned, primitive dance of joy. "Isaiah dances, Isaiah dances before the Lord. . . ." A song living when the world was young, older than Christianity, old only as Isaiah who in the Bible was too staid to dance.[1]

Then out we went again into the sunshine, across the fields to the bridegroom's house, which was now Ilinca's home The women took her in and dressed her in the matron's long veil of white linen reaching to her heels. Round and round went the ţuica, and the yard was full of dancing.

Untiringly we danced. The next six days would be hard and given to labour.

"It will be your turn next, Anica. I have seen you."

"What will she do with marriage," grumbled an old woman over the cooking-pots. "Anica indeed ! She has too many lovers."

So Anica is fickle, is she? Do you wish, old women that you had her slim waist, bright cheeks, and dark, dancing eyes? Anica is only what you have been, and will be what you are, what all of you must be. You dance and in the week you work, and then you marry and bear children and work on till your faces are the colour of the earth. A life of labour. The sun parches the crops, the rain drowns them. After the snowbound winter the spring passes as soon as it has come. Dance and laugh and love ! There are no other pleasures where life depends on sun and rain.

In springtime the girls go to the river and pray that they may have beauty, make incantations as their mothers and grandmothers have made before them. Those incantations succeed, for see how beautiful they are— beautiful as their prayers.

"Bathed in this precious water I shall become sweet with the scent of basil, and beautiful, O star of all the stars, as you are beautiful."

With the going down of the sun the tables were once more spread, and we sat down to another feasting. The musicians were indefatigable.

> Hill is hill and valley, valley,
> My love is mine until she dies.
> Once you were your mother's daughter,
> But now, love, you are married.

> If my sweetheart were the moon
> I would see her evermore;
> But sweetheart it's a long road,
> Without my book I cannot go.

---

[1] In spite of considerable research I cannot discover the origin of this song. It is an old hymn taken from the Greek service book 'When did Isaiah dance?'

First I could not mark my book
As the headman was not well,
Then the notary was angry
When I marked the book all wrong.

Sweetheart, say, what shall I do?

And they all laughed; they have to carry little passports if they go on a journey. The country is close to Russia and their Government has to watch for agents of the Soviet. But it is like them to make a song and a joke about it.

The moon came up and we danced on. But I was becoming very sleepy. Costica, too, was tired and we had six miles over the hills to walk. Coming together at a pause in the dancing we went to find the bridegroom to say good-bye. But he had disappeared and the bride as well. The dancing could do without them and they without the dancing.

So we went home in the moonlight. Soon the music had died away behind us and we were alone in the soft night. The silence of the hills was on us. We ran no more and did not sing, only seldom did we speak. For the music still sang in our ears, and the *ţuica* hummed a little in our brains. Sometimes we lay down on the warm earth. Once we fell asleep, and when we opened our eyes the moon was low down. In the valleys it had disappeared.

The foolish cocks were crowing at the false dawn when we came to the village. Later in Moraştio, when the sun was up, the boys took Ilinca and Ilie's marriage sheet and waved it rejoicing through the lanes, for there was a red stain on it that proved to them that Ilie had been Inlinca's first love.

CHAPTER 7

HUSKING OF CORN

◆

Now the harvesting was nearly done. From the stripped fields came the heavy ox-carts, rumbling ponderously through the lanes and down the village street. Light clouds of dust hung above the mountains of corn-cobs as they were emptied into the yards and open barns. Along the ways lay the dried sheaths where they had fallen. Some of the peasants more forward with the work of harvesting were already in the fields with their sickles slashing at the naked cornstalks. In the wheat stubble were multitudes of geese honking their pleasure at their rich gleaning.

There was no rest now. The long, dry summer had made the harvest poor. Everything must be gathered, to the last ear and cob, if the people were to be fed through the hard winter. Men, women, and children were all day working; yet at night, tired as they were, there were always songs and laughter while the weary children slept in the corners of the rooms.

As we plodded homeward the sun hung low down behind the trees, leaving the evening drowsy with the heat of its fiery trail across the sky. But there was a haze over the fields, a gentle serenity in the air; the sad sweetness of summer's passing enveloped the whole earth. Twilight, as it deepened, came now not with summer's passion and dark heat, but with sleepy caress that told of the long sleep in store. And when night came it was fresh, quickening the limbs for the day's toil. The moon shone clear and cold.

"Soon," said Nicolaie Dumitrescu, "we shall have the curățat."[1]

"Curățat?" I asked, straightening myself from the task of loading a cart and wiping the sweat from my face.

"The husking of the corn. To-morrow night, or perhaps the night after, Gheorghe Tamaș will have gathered all his corn. All the village will go to help him clean it. Soon all the corn will be in, then every night there will be a curățat. You will see."

So, when a few nights later as I leaned on the rail outside the house I heard the sound of music, I guessed what it meant. For a little while I did not move. There was no one about, and but for the distant lilting the night was quiet. Standing there I let the sense of my remoteness grow till I seemed

---

[1] Pronounced curatsat.

to drift out of myself. It is my way, perhaps a lazy one, of allowing a sensation to leave its impress on me. I hardly think that I am conscious of what I am at. But there are times when a silence becomes pregnant of beauty for me, so that with the sharpening of my senses my mind becomes subconsciously acutely receptive. I know that it is receptive only because I remember so fully afterwards. At the time it seems numb. That distant, formless music was welling up from the heart of the land, the perennial rejoicing at the gathering of corn which meant life to the people till it came again at the next turn of the year. The very faintness of the music, which at times quite died away leaving utter silence, seemed to be reaching back to the beginning of things when men first learned to sow the seed that gave them life.

Footsteps shuffling in the thick dust of the roadway paused at the gate.

"Nicolaie Dumitrescu," called a man's voice.

"Nicolaie is not here." I answered. "I think he has gone to the *cură̦tat*."

"Ah, it is you, *domnule Englez*. And Costica?"

"He has gone too, I think. There is no one here."

"Are you not coming?"

"Yes, soon."

"Good ! I will see you then."

The man passed on. I waited while the silence came again. Then, as a burst of singing swelled into the night, I went down the steps and out into the road. The moon shone clearly, whitening the way, the shadows under the trees were black. The houses, cleanly outlined, looked asleep. Only the dogs heard me and barked suddenly as I passed the gateways. Had I not known Gheorghe Tamaş's house the music would have deceived me. For it rose and fell so strangely that sometimes it seemed right at my ear and at other times sounded from far away.

At the entrance to Gheorghe's yard I paused a moment in the shadows. Along one side of it stood his house, and across the moonlit yard facing the roadway was a barn open on one side. On its wall was a lamp throwing into grotesque relief the men and women crowded on a vast heap of corncobs. In a corner two *ţigani*[1] made music, one, with a fiddle, was standing singing and swaying, the other, half-hidden, plucked at a lute. The movements of the huskers as they tore the cobs free from the sheaths and threw them out on the growing pile in the yard made a symphony of dark, dancing shadows.

As I crossed the yard a voice called:

"Here is *domnule Englez*."

And Nicolaie Dumitrescu said:

[1] Pronounced tsiganey

44

"We thought you would be tired, so we came alone."

"Tired ! "laughed a woman. "He has come for the pretty girls and the dancing."

"Then he should have rested himself."

"I shall enjoy them more if I work first," I answered as I sat down on the heap and began to tear at the sheathed cobs.

The ţigan with the fiddle, a tall, thin man with the face of a clown, bowed quizzically to me and broke into a ridiculous song which he accompanied with terrible grimaces:

> Mr. Englishman has come to us
> Because he is so lonely.
> Looking at the moonlit night
> He longed so for his wife
> That he went running down the street
> To try and find a lady.
> In this village there are girls
> More lovely than the flowers,
> He will soon forget his wife
> When he starts to dance !

"Oi ! Oi !" he shouted, bursting with exaggerated laughter. "See how sad he looks. His forehead is dark like heavy, winter clouds." Leaning forward he took a bottle of ţuica from one of the men and tipped it to his mouth. "Ah ! That will do him good."

He thrust the bottle toward me and I drank to his health. With a darting smile, as though apologizing for his rough joking, he was off again on another tune.

But never for a moment did the work flag. Sometimes when the ţigani played a favourite song, we beat time with the corn cobs. The chatter and the singing went on while the heap on which we sat sank lower and lower as the pile of naked cobs mounted in the yard. Round and round went the ţuica, merrier and merrier were the workers.

> Then comes autumn, rich with vintage,
> Happily the world rejoices,
> He who works will want for nothing
> When the heavy winter falls.

sang the ţigan. Then lest anyone should think he was becoming serious, he roared with laughter and, throwing down his fiddle, began to act a two part comedy, changing his voice back and forth from a deep bass to a thin falsetto while his companion strummed an accompaniment.

Ten, eleven, twelve o'clock, the hours slipped by. Many of the people had been at the husking for two hours before I had come. Sure Gheorghe Tamaş would have enough and to spare for his mamaliga and his bread. But the fun and good humour never abated. What they were doing for Gheorghe Tamaş to-night he and others would be doing for them for many nights to come. No money passes for the labour but to the ţigani. Gheorghe was paying for them; and we were there to help him, hired for the songs, for the pleasure of gathering together in good company and for the dancing presently. To-morrow night one of us will be paying the ţigani, while Gheorghe comes with his family to help another's husking. So it will go on all round the village till every one's corn is safely unsheathed and stored. Then will come the long winter, a waiting while the seed germinates in the earth and grows to another harvest. Thus will the cycle of the years and of their lives be rounded.

"*Domnule Englez*, you have a watch, what is the time? "

"One o'clock."

"It is nearly done. Quick, quick ! Oh, you lazy ones in the corner, are you going to sleep? Hurry, or the moon will be gone."

Now it was over. In the barn lay only a trampled heap of husks. Outside the golden cobs were a mountainous pile. The fiddlers had moved out into the moonlit yard and in the middle were slipping into a vigorous *hora*.

Two men were already dancing, arms on each other's shoulders, their feet twinkling in intricate steps. Who to see these people dance would dream that all day they moved heavily on the earth? The music transforms them; these are no clodhoppers, their feet move as lightly as a ballet dancer's. Da-dana, da-dana, soon more joined in; the line grew longer circling about the fiddlers, but never the two ends touched.

Into the centre ran a man, glanced a moment around, and then chose his partner, whirling her nearly off her feet as he seized her around the waist. Then another and another, till at a shout from the ţigani we all changed partners.

There was no sad, slow music. No songs to remind the dancers of their labour, of the long years of oppression under hard taskmasters. Every one was free, the music cried it, throbbing with the joy of living. A night of rejoicing with only the moonlight cold on the flushed faces of the dancers.

I could feel the blood beating faster in my veins. Round and round I went; my arm was tight around the waist of Anica, then Pipina, then

Smaranda.

"*Domnule Englez*, how did you learn to dance our dances?"

How did I learn? Who could not dance on such a night? Had I not been with these people in the fields, felt the strong surge of strength as day after day I had grown with them closer to the earth? I had learned from them their power over the earth and the earth's power over them, learned the balance of power which came with their knowledge of the earth's every move and its consummation with the sun and rain. This music was a part of them, and, as I had grown to know them, I understood their music. It was not necessary to remember the airs; that I could never do. Springing from a single source they were too alike in their fundamentals, too diverse in their infinite variations. The music flows from the fingers of the *ţigani*, through their fiddles, and out into the air. How, with that moon shining and all around me swaying to the music, could I resist its surging, compelling force? The rhythm thrilled me and I danced because I had to.

Then because I did not wish to see it end I slipped away. There came a pause. The people broke up into groups, talking and laughing. In the shadows I saw Costica with Pipina's hand in his; they were not speaking but their heads were close. All at once that same hopeless feeling came to me as it had done when years before I had lived with the Indians in New Mexico. Why persuade myself that I could ever be a part of what surrounded me? With the affection of these people I could learn their customs, their language, even know themselves. But that other thing, the unseen essence that was their soul, that I could never probe. They were apart from me, their joys and sorrows, though I might think that I understood them, were of a wholly different nature from mine. I might love the earth, but I could not comprehend its language as could they who were a part of it.

I became suddenly lonely. Even now if I left their dancing they would not miss me. The fiddles had struck up again. I edged into the shadows and passed out through the gateway into the road. The music grew fainter till as I reached the house it had died quite away. Even the watchdog slept. The silence was complete. Pipina was with Costica, Smaranda was with . . . Anica as with . . . And I, well perhaps after all I felt as I did because I was in love with some one who was far away. Anyway I felt very tired.

In the morning Nicolaie said:

"Why did you go so early? We were sorry that you did not stay to the end."

And with the sunlight glancing over the stubble I rejoiced absurdly at the thought that perhaps I really had been missed.

CHAPTER 8

THE MAN WHO BREATHED DREAMS

◆

About a week later when we were in the fields there was a sense of dull foreboding. The people moved heavily and slowly at their work, pausing frequently to look up at the sky. Not a leaf stirred, no bird sang. Voices from distant fields carried sonorously. The lowing of cattle from the water-meadows was persistent and melancholy. Towards midday tumbled clouds gathered on the horizon, the sun grew dull as though a curtain had been stretched over the sky. The heat became increasingly oppressive.

"It is coming," they said, looking around them at the field now almost cleared of its crop.

A light, warm wind began to blow; as it grew in force clouds of dust were swept up from the parched earth, along the white road they rose in whirling columns. Feverishly now we went to work, for no one knew how long the storm would last. The trees bent and sobbed, shaking and quivering at the tearing gusts, from the forests on the hillsides came a soughing, moaning cry. Overhead slateand coppercoloured clouds drove across the sun, darkening the earth. The lightning flashes came at ever-shortening intervals, while the thunder grew in tremendous volume. Then, with a wild screaming, the storm broke. Across the fields it swept in a wall of glistening silver, drowning sight. Hailstones danced and bounced on the earth, falling so thickly that the fields were pebbled with white. Crouching beneath the carts, our heated bodies chilled by the all-saturating rain, we waited for the first fury of the storm to pass. But the wind grew ever stronger, driving before it the clusters of naked sheaves, even hurling the piled cobs from the cart.

"It will last long,"
they said. "There will be no more work to-day."

Bending our heads to the storm we returned to the village, the oxen plodding uncomplaining under the heavy load, the water pouring from their steaming sides.

All night the gale lasted, but towards dawn it slackened and there was only the sound of water running in a thousand channels. For two days the rain fell steadily; on the third it had passed. The sky was stainless, the whole world had been washed clean. The air was clear, the earth glistened, and the trees shone with a brighter green in defiance of the autumn which threatened to turn their colour. It was as though all creation had been changed to one great diamond.

The rain had come too late to do either good or harm and the crops were now soon gathered in. With the great part of the work over I again sometimes explored the country round. One day as I was walking through an orchard on the hills to the east of the village I came upon a number of peasants gathering the fruit.

"You will have much țuica," I said, looking around at the laden trees.

"It is not ours. It belongs to the doctor."

As I stood there a man came up the hill towards us. He was of middle height, well-built, and with a short pointed beard. I judged him to be about sixty. He wore dark, country tweeds and a broad-brimmed, black hat. The peasant who was with him said something and he glanced up. Raising his hat he came up to me and took my hand.

"This is a pleasure. I had heard that there was an Englishman in the village. I am glad to have met you."

I apologized for trespassing in his orchard and he laughed.

"This is Romania. Every one goes where he pleases. Have you seen how țuica is made? Come with me and I will show you."

So we went down together, the doctor knocking the plums from the trees and filling my hands with them. In a barn were eight enormous barrels about ten feet high, standing on their ends. A gentle sizzling came from them, the air was filled with the scent of fermenting plums.

"When I make țuica I do not make it straight from the fruit off the trees as the peasants do. I fill these barrels and let the plums lie there fermenting for about six weeks. After that I put them in the fabrica. That is in the other shed. There are some there now."

I had no idea that țuica could be made so simply. On a brick furnace stood a large copper, a long pipe from it led through a barrel and from the pipe's end fell drop by drop the țuica into a container.

"It is primitive, is it not? The fermenting plums are put in the copper, the vapour passes through the pipe. In that barrel is water which is always cold because a stream from the hill flows through it. So the vapour is condensed and there is țuica. So simple, eh?"

He looked at his watch.

"Will you excuse me if I go now? My wife is awaiting me. Perhaps you will lunch with me to-morrow."

I said that I had no decent clothes.

"That does not matter. We are not grand people. Is there anything special you would like to eat? I am sure the food you have with Pițigoiu[1] is very rough."

Pițigoiu means tom-tit and was the nickname given to Nicolaie Dumitrescu because he talked so fast that it was hard even for the villagers to understand what he said.

"Whatever you give me will be good. But if you do not mind my saying so I would prefer not to have mamaliga. I have been living on it."

He laughed. "Mamaliga ! Brrr ! Living on it, eh? You have indeed given your stomach to the devil. No, I promise you you shall not have mamaliga."

I have never eaten such a meal as I did the next day; and that is saying a good deal of a meal in a country whose people are the most prodigious eaters perhaps in the world. Though capacities might increase everywhere if food became as plentiful and cheap as it is in Romania. We had first ciorba de pui, a sour soup made from chicken, rich with butter and filled with vegetables. This was followed by a sucking pig. It came on to the table whole, half an apple in its mouth, a blue bow on its forehead. I felt sad till I began to eat it, and then my sorrow passed. This seemed to me to be enough. But then came slices of roast goose with peppers, and afterwards a cheese pancake. The wine was good too.

"It is from Drăgășani,"[2] said the doctor. "The wine here is not good. We are too near the mountains, for a great part of the year the nights are cold so the grapes are small and sour. Noroc !"

We raised our glasses and drank to his wife's health.

It was very peaceful there sitting on the veranda. Below us was the village almost hidden in the trees, and beyond the hills rose gently, low, rolling hills naked now of their golden crops. To the north they climbed in forested masses to the high, blue line of the Carpathians. My companions were a charming, though oddly assorted couple. He, shrewd and quiet, with dark, sparkling eyes which were almost closed when he laughed, she plump, round-eyed and a little untidy, very talkative, speaking in a quick, jerky manner which made it difficult for me to understand her.

"It is gentle here, is it not? " said the doctor. "Simpatic. As you know, I am a Greek. But I have lived here for thirty years. Only last year I retired from being the district doctor."

"Do you not go back to your country at all?"

He shrugged his shoulders.

---

[1] Pronounced pitsigoi   [2] Pronounced Dragashan.

"When I came here I was young, now I am old. . . ."

"Do not listen to my foolish husband," gabbled his wife.

"Old indeed, he stays here because he likes it. Why do you think he married me, a Romanian? Because he loves Romania of course—and all the girls. You should see his eyes sparkle. Old !"

The doctor laughed indulgently.

"It is true. Though not about the girls—oh, no. The longer you stay in this country the more difficult it is to leave. In thirty years I have only returned to Greece five times. When I came here first I was thirty-two, and before that I had travelled to many countries. For a time my family lived in Turkey. But always after a while I became lonely. Here I have never felt that, even at the beginning. The people are so kindly, if you are sad they understand. Simpatic. That is the word, the whole country is simpatic. Look now before you. Would you change anything of that?"

And looking over the quiet valley at the hills, I knew what he said was true.

"Of course," he went on, speaking slowly and at times turning to French for my assistance. "You and I see the peasants in a different way. I have long ceased to be a foreigner, and also have never lived with them. In fact, but for you, I have never met any one who has. I am to them just a landowner, like any of their boyars. They raise their hats to me and call me ' sir '. I do not know the intimate side of their lives. Neither do the boyars know it. For so many years have the peasants been in servitude that such a thing is impossible. The only bridge between them is their love of their country. But Romania has been united for so short a time that the link is not yet felt. I know only that they are a happy, good-humoured people."

I told him that it was their good-humour that had impressed me most of all. Often I had listened to them baiting one another in the most infuriating way, but they never lost their heads.

"That is so, their patience is wonderful. But once they have passed it . . ." He threw out a hand expressively. "In the war I was in the medical service. I was at the terrible battle of Mărăşeşti.[1] As you know it was the last great battle of the war in Romania. Mackensen had an army equipped with every modern weapon. He meant to crush us. Those peasants fought like madmen. The Russians deserted us, and we had to close up the gaps till there was only a long, thin line. But Mackensen could not get past the peasants. It is true that the peasants are Romania.

"When I came here I could not speak a word of their language. But they seemed to know exactly how to teach me. They joke at my mistakes, but they take great care to explain where I am wrong and insist that I get a

[1] Pronounced Marashesht

52

sentence perfect. That is intelligence.

"They are the most intelligent peasants I have ever known. That is why the country is content. It is dreadfully poor, but there is no unrest. The peasant knows that since he has been given his land it is his own fault if he starves. We are next door to Russia, but communism has not a chance; the peasants laugh at it. They know well enough when they are well off. Of course they complain. What peasant in any country does not? 'criza mǎre, criza mǎre,' they say, but the great crisis does not touch them. Look at the house I am building." He pointed to the shell of a structure which stood in a clump of trees farther down the hill. "I started on it last year, and there it is only halffinished now. I cannot get any one to work on it, every one is too busy. There is almost no unemployment in this country. Every man either owns or has relations who own land to which he goes if he cannot find work. Perhaps my house will be finished next summer."

"Meanwhile it is a monument to your patience."

"Patience ! "broke in his wife. "He has no patience. It is just that time does not exist here."

"You hear her," said the doctor. "Yet I shall have waited two years for my house. But she is right, there is no time."

"Then you have solved a great problem."

"No, I am too lazy to worry."

"Or have found out what constitutes happiness."

He was silent a moment, toying with his wineglass. His wife had gone into the house to sleep, for it was hot.

"Are you a philosopher?" he asked suddenly.

"My brain is too muddled."

"All philosophers start with muddled brains, that is what makes them philosophers. When you have met my friend Stavrache, the boyar, after whom this village was named, you will see what I mean. Have you met many Russians?"

"No."

"He has the mind rather of a Russian. Many of the cultured boyars have. An over-intellectualized brain given to sudden fancies, to phantom paths that lead nowhere. You have read Tolstoi and Dostoevski? "

"Yes."

"Then you will be prepared. Presently when . . ."

His voice died away and he half-closed his eyes, his hand lying still by his glass.

"I have often thought," I said, "that if I could be long enough alone, I could, by the lack of distraction, allow the impressions that I have received consciously and subconsciously to form themselves into a pattern that would give me some key to the seemingly haphazard existence we lead. Yet I believe that to do that deliberately would lay oneself open to even the smallest form of distraction, whereas here life seems to move in the people as an undercurrent that would not rise to disturb suddenly the surface on which I drifted. There would then be always life beneath my contemplation. What do you think?"

There was a long silence. I turned my head expectantly. The doctor was asleep.

Well, I was not surprised. And laughed inwardly at the thought of how soothing, or boring, my suggestion of contemplation must have been. What had led me to this train of thought? Perhaps the sudden relaxation from the toil of the past weeks when my mind must in truth have been working steadily beneath the surface of the mechanical direction it gave to my body.

I waited. A fly settled on the doctor's cheek, but he did not stir. His head was sunk forward, his beard pressing on his waistcoat. So I tiptoed quietly away and went to look at his pigs routing in the field, queer, half-wild creatures with long, curly hair which at a distance made them look like sheep. I was not away long, and when I returned the doctor had not moved. So, since I could not leave him, I sat down under a tree with him in view. For a while my mind stirred lazily. I closed my eyes; each time that I opened them to look at the doctor the effort became greater. The bees droned heavily.

I was awakened by a laugh. The doctor was standing over me.

"You let me sleep and slept yourself. That is the penalty of indulgence."

"*Made* you sleep," I said. "All the same, it is your fault for giving me such an excellent lunch."

"Now that we are rested, and it is cooler, shall we walk down and call on my friend Stavrache?"

"That is a splendid idea."

The boyar's house was about two miles away in the valley on the outskirts of the village. I had passed it several times, but had had no idea that it was the home of the man whose family had once owned the village for hundreds of years. In fact, I had wondered if it was deserted. It stood far back from the road, a massive, square, stone building with nakedlooking windows staring out over a rambling and ill-kept garden surrounded by a high wall. To one side of it were a number of outbuildings of all shapes and sizes, mostly in bad repair. As we entered the gateway and went up the drive a wolf-hound came tearing across the grass at us baying furiously.

"Iancu, Iancu, come here, beast," shouted a peasant emerging from one of the outhouses. He picked up a handful of stones and began to hurl them at the animal, which fled angrily. "He is savage, that one. Yes, domnul Stavrache is at home."

We went up the steps to the front door and rang the bell. I could hear it pealing somewhere in the recesses of the house. Then came the sound of shuffling feet and the door was opened by an old woman. The hall was long and bare, stone-flagged, the only piece of furniture a deal table piled high with papers. The air was chill and musty.

At the sound of our voices the boyar came towards us from a room on the left of the hall his hand outstretched. He was a heavily built man of about fifty-five. His head was massive, his eyes, deep-set beneath thick eyebrows, looked hazy as though he was short-sighted, until he spoke, when they became keen and bright. He had a wide moustache and a long, thin nose strangely at variance with his other features which were rather coarse. His mouth was large and his lips curled sensually.

"Ah, the doctor. And your friend?" He turned, bowing slightly, and to my surprise addressed me in English. "You are the Englishman of whom I have heard. Do you like my village? Come this way."

His voice was deep and cultured; he spoke slowly, rounding his words as though savouring their richness. So that his every remark, however trivial, took on a weight which commanded attention.

The room into which he led us was large, though all sense of space was lost on account of the heavy furniture which filled it. In one corner stood an immense stove, big enough for a man to lie on and covered with blue tiles. In another a stained deal cupboard jutted out into the room. In a third corner and stretching along the wall was an ugly iron bedstead. The table filling the centre of the room was covered with an embroidered tablecloth heavily fringed. Long, dark curtains hung at the windows, making the light dreary. Two arm-chairs of the last century had white antimacassars over their backs. Stavrache brought forward some stiff, plush-covered chairs and placed them by the table.

"Please be seated," he said. "You will have Turkish coffee?" He called to the old woman and gave the order.

"I am reading the memoirs of the Duchess d'Abrantes," he said, lifting a book from the table. "She lived in a stirring age. This is a dull one. Though the people think it is upset enough. My English, it is not very good. Though I read it much I have not spoken it for ten years. You will excuse me if I sometimes speak Romanian, or the doctor will not understand."

I told him that he spoke excellently, but that I already knew some

Romanian. He seemed delighted at that and went on sometimes in one language, sometimes in the other.

"You are here to study the peasants? That is funny. Ha ! What do you think of them—dirty?"

"Well, yes, I suppose they are. But in a way that is not unpleasant. It is earthy dirt, not like the dirt of a town. And there are many compensations."

"True. But you have no bed, no mattress?"

"No, only straw. Now I have become used to it, it is quite comfortable. Though I wish there was more of it."

"The more straw, the more purici."[1]

I told him that the purici had not bitten me after the first night as they must have all died of overeating. He laughed richly at that.

"But tell me what you think of the peasants. Seriously, I should like to know."

"I am very fond of them. They are good-natured, intelligent, and I believe they have a sense of beauty."

"I have heard some landowners say they were too intelligent," said the doctor, drawing his hand over his beard. Then he was silent again, his eyes twinkling, his hands resting on his knees.

Stavrache too was silent for a moment. Then he leaned forward with a sudden intensity, speaking with deep precision, as though taking each word, holding it before him, and turning it to the light before he used it.

"A sense of beauty is a rare thing. In many countries the peasant has been sentimentalized, he has been represented as being not only a lover of nature but a lover of beauty in nature. I hold that this is much exaggerated, particularly in Western Europe. The peasant is not unconscious of this beauty, but it has not significant influence on him. What does move him is something deeper, something which a civilized individual does not feel. I mean the constant relationship of himself to the earth, the parallel which he unconsciously draws between his own life and that of the earth and all growing things. He is in most countries a high type of animal."

"That may be due to the increasing impress of civilization on him," I said. "Civilization and education in the first instance do harm. Its first effect is to make a man dissatisfied with what he has without giving him anything tangible in its place. He becomes ashamed of what has always meant much to him, what has moved him through his senses."

"It is beginning here. But our peasants have an instinct for beauty. I do not believe that they think about it at all. And because of that it will pass. Not for many generations, but the evil of vulgarity will creep into their blood and will pass from parents to children, always growing stronger,

---

[1] Pronounced pooreechy

even as it has in other countries where the sense of beauty is not so great. It is starting now in the villages that are near to towns. What do you think?"

"I am thinking of the colour harmonies in the peasant clothes. There is never a mistake."

Stavrache took a sip at his thick, Turkish coffee, smacking his lips.

"True. But you have seen what a peasant buys in a shop if he has any money?"

"Something hideous."

"Quite so. That is because he is also a child. He is told that an article is fine. Since it is new to him he believes the shopman. He does not think about its lack of beauty, but it interests him like a new toy. That is the evil. Do you know that German manufacturers can send stuff to this country so cheaply that it costs less than the materials used by some of the peasants, who live near the towns, in making their own clothes? It is horrible. The price of beauty is high."

"Do you mean that you can buy it?"

"Of course. But not here. Listen to me. In most civilized people the instinct for beauty has disappeared, they have been educated out of it. The world is vulgar; no period has so vulgarized it as the last hundred years." He raised his finger. "An artist knows the worth of his work and charges accordingly. So we have allowed money the monopoly of procuring beauty. A manufacturer will not pay its price when he knows that he can sell his tawdry goods, without paying an artist designer, to millions who are as debased in taste as he is himself. So he proceeds to debase them further. The world is the slave of money. Here there is no money, so for the time being we are saved. Nothing of interest has happened since the French Revolution." He paused. "Do you believe in God?"

Rising from his chair he went to sit on the edge of his bed, looking moodily across at the doctor who was idly turning the pages of the book.

"You must stay to supper. The doctor is bored, which means he is hungry."

"No, no," said the doctor, "I have been listening. But you are all wrong. As medical adviser to the world I should suggest rigid birth control and sterilization. More people, more vulgarity. Less people, more room to develop naturally."

Stavrache threw back his massive heard and laughed harshly. "What nonsense you talk. You have not heard a word of what I have been saying."

Opening the door, he shouted, "Madalina !"

"Coming, *domnule*," sounded the old woman's voice.

"Madalina, the gentlemen are staying to supper."

"But, domnule . . ."

Stavrache went out and shut the door.

"It is always the same," said the doctor. "There is never any food in the house. God knows how he lives. I will go, or there will not be enough. But you must stay or he will be hurt. He is very proud. This is almost the only room that is furnished; he reads, eats, and sleeps in here. Once he was rich, but he managed everything so badly that now he has lost nearly all his money."

When Stavrache returned the doctor rose.

"I really must go. I promised my wife that I would return an hour ago."

"But I have ordered supper for you. Are you sure you cannot stay?" He eyed the doctor quizzically, struggling between pride and relief.

"Yes. But domnul Hall will be more entertained without me. I am dull company."

"I shall be charmed to accept your invitation," I said.

The boyar smiled graciously.

"Ah, well, that is good. Then another time, doctor."

When we returned from seeing the doctor to the gate a lamp was lit and the table laid. We sipped țuica and waited while Madalina prepared supper:

"He is a good fellow, the doctor. I do not know what I should do without him. The other people of property around here are of no interest to me. Rich and stupid, nouveaux riches, but fortunately there are only three of them."

Madalina brought in soup and fried chicken. We followed up with pancakes and some fine ewes' cheese. A good supper I thought. Stavrache ate in the same manner as he spoke, slowly and delicately, savouring each morsel. I noticed how shapely were his hands, slim-fingered and with well-kept nails. There was about him an air of authority, of centuries of fine breeding which was accentuated by the drabness of his surroundings. He spoke little during the meal, and, thinking that I might feel that he was not entertaining me, said:

"There are few pleasures in life. It is therefore foolish to spoil appreciation of one by trying to combine it with another. I eat much alone, but I never read at my meals. So, when I have company I do not talk unless I know that I shall not be able to later. Do you understand?"

"Completely."

We finished in silence. When Madalina had cleared the table and we were once more drinking the inevitable Turkish coffee Stavrache went to a bureau and laid before me a crinkled parchment.

"That is the confirmation of my family in its estates. It is two hundred years old. My family had owned them for three hundred years before that was granted. But it is interesting, is it not?"

Before I had time to examine it he rolled it up again.

"Who do I show it to you? It is simply pride. And of what have I to be proud? The peasants now have nearly all my land. They have a vote each, while I still have only one. There are times when I hate the peasants," he said bitterly. And I saw from the sensual curl of his lips that he had also inherited a cruel arrogance that was dying of impotence. "It is only because I know in myself that it is the peasants who have made Romania that allows me to suffer them. We, the boyars, have no instinct for government; it is natural for us - *laissez-faire*. In the past, when we were fighting to be free from the Turks or the Russians or the Magyars, we fought only for ourselves - that is excepting a few great ones. But the peasants fought for their very earth. It is they who freed the land. Now because we are still lazy a crowd of filthy, self-seeking politicians rule; there are one or two good men, the rest are disgusting, canaille. I know what the rest of Europe thinks of Romania. I read the foreign newspapers." As he walked slowly up and down the room he kicked a pile in the corner. "It laughs at her. Your country laughs more than any other."

"It laughs because it is ignorant," I said apologetically.

"The laughter of the ignorant is the vilest of all." His voice rose for the fist time. "The Press is the ruination of the world. Here is a land, freed at last from oppression, peopled as you have seen with men and women who, though backward, are beautiful and intelligent. They are backward because for centuries they have been tossed between the West and the East. Now, because they are led by scamps, they are gibed at. This land would be Utopia if it were well governed." He checked himself and grumbled angrily, "Manners have died since the French Revolution."

"Suppose that they have," I said. "Some of us have ceased to dream falsely."

He halted in his walk and came and sat down opposite me.

"Ah, you do not admire the Romantics."

I had only meant to turn the conversation from politics which did not interest me, and for the moment felt baffled. But Stavrache did not wait for an answer.

"You speak of dreams. But the world is as our selfconsciousness makes it, and only the genius, the constructive artist, knows the true self. The world is the dream of our inner life. Emotions, experiences of the heart and soul alone teach us to understand it. Schelling knew this, he knew that as the heart changes so much the view of the world and therefore the conception of what is worth while change. The laws of nature are allied to the laws of the heart. Feeling is an essential guide to reason. Schlegel before he deserted the Romantics said that the deepest truth he knew was that his present truth would change. That is true wisdom."

"Yes," I broke in. "But he said that just because the world was for him only of the heart, and, as you say, the heart changes often."

"You are here because you love nature. You must be or you would not care to lead such a life as you do here. Then you must agree with Schelling's *Naturphilosophie*. It is not the facts of nature that are important, it is your understanding of nature through your senses. To be emotionally stirred is to comprehend. Man evolves from nature. Spirit comes to man after it has been first expressed in nature. ' *Ich bin der Gott der sie im Busen trägt.*' You understand? Yes? But you do not feel it?" As he peered steadfastly at me the short-sighted look came into his eyes, as though he was indeed not seeing me but some inward vision. His full lips were pursed, he breathed heavily through his nose. Then his face brightened. "To understand fully one must be emotionally stirred; I have said that. The scientists pile up what they call facts; they feel nothing. Other scientists discover more facts which displace the first, which were of course no more facts than those which displaced them; so it goes on, on, on. . . . The Romantics knew their unreliability and so will always be greater. They knew the fickleness of nature. But in rare moments of emotion they discovered what no scientist could ever find. It is the poet who knows the meaning of life, the lover who sees its heart. No man who has not been in love can understand why the flowers grow towards the sun. But when he has, then only can he know."

I felt the ecstatic waves closing over my head; in a moment I should be lost in the deep persuasiveness of his voice. I pressed my hand to my forehead trying to rescue my drowning reason. The effort too of following the argument sometimes in Romanian, sometimes in English, was intense.

"But feelings must have facts to support them," I said. "The Romantics were not only emotional, they were sentimental. They made themselves feel for the sake of feeling. If they had lasted the value of their experience would have been lost. Idealism without an objective foundation can be harmful. From feelings can come the lowest as well as the highest things. You may have the beauty of Schelling, but at a later extreme you have the horrors of Poe."

"What?" ejaculated Stavrache, his lips quivering with half-formed worlds. But for the last time I would have my say.

"A knowledge of history and a real understanding of its significance is a thing of value that sprang from the Romantics. They loved passion and mystery, and sought for it in the Orient and the Middle Ages. They did not at first connect what they found with the history of humanity, but they stimulated the interest. Later, those who had been dreamers changed their views when they saw that the present was only a minute in evolution. They began to see that laws and customs however primitive, were of human worth, and that the meaning of life could not be summed up in a single sensation. Germany was chaotic; there was no room for the Romantics on the earth, so they lived in the air. But that state did not last. Those who followed realized, as they studied history, that every generation depends upon former generations. That our ideals are not a gift from above, but the outcome of centuries of struggle, of effort that is often blind. Superstition, cruelty, hunger, toil, the most unideal forces combine to form our ideals."

"Ah ! But every one thinks that now. You would say it is obvious." Stavrache went gloomily to his bed, which seemed to give him some kind of comfort, and sat down, gnawing his fingers. "But instinct has always a greater say than reason. Do not forget that."

"That is different," I said. "But if your world of sensation, of experience, is as real as you say it is then its reality must be deeper than our experience."

I felt played out. The night was stuffy, all the windows were shut and the lamp smelt abominably. Stavrache was apparently indifferent to all these things; his large face was now expressionless, he seemed sunk within himself. I rose from my chair, fearful that the thoughts that were stirring behind that mask would spring out on me again. Stavrache passed his large, slender hand over his face, drawing it from forehead to chin. When he glanced up he was once more smiling.

"You are tired," he said, coming towards me. "I must apologize. That I have not often the chance to talk so much must be my excuse. We will perhaps continue the discussion later, eh? " He laid his hand on my arm. "You are young; do not waste your life in speculation or you may find yourself living in an airless world, breathing only your dreams."

But for the solemnity of his voice I could have laughed. In trust, I felt almost sick in the airlessness of his room. Holding out my hand I moved towards the door. Stavrache took a lantern.

"I will see you to the road," he said.

At the gate he halted.

"All the evening there has been in my mind a question so strongly fixed that I do not know if I have asked it. Do you believe in God?"

"I should be glad if some one could convince me that there is one."

"Ah !" He paused, and the lantern dangling from his hand threw heavy shadows above the sensual curl of his lips. That shall be our thesis. Good night." With that he turned on his heel and left me.

I drew great draughts of air into my lungs as I went homeward. With each step I felt lighter, and wondered how it was that I had become suddenly so near to fainting in that room. Perhaps it was that dreams had indeed filled it.

CHAPTER 9

FEASTING THE DEAD

◆

After that evening I met Stavrache several times. But, though he was always courteous, he never attempted a serious discussion. I do not know if he wished afterwards that he had not opened out so to a stranger. I asked the doctor about him, and he told me that in his youth the boyar had lived much abroad, mostly in Paris, squandering his fortune. But for the last fifteen years he had not left his estate, which had grown smaller and smaller. He hardly ever went out, and spent all his time reading.

Maria, when I told her where I had been, said that she was glad.

"He is lonely. He has no one to love, no wife, no children. And what is life without children? When he dies it is the end of him here."

Fertility was a strong point with Maria. She adored her children too. Though the blind love which all these people have for their children and their persistent desire to have more is quite foolish. They pet and spoil them and give them everything they want. The things I saw Maria give her baby Dorina to eat because she thought she would like them made me shudder. Hundreds die of a surfeit of affection—more, I should think than die of a complete lack of hygiene. It makes them cry terribly if they are left alone. Dorina gave me an awful time.

Most of the villages felt the same about Stavrache. A few of them despised him, and I believe feared him a little. But he had almost nothing to do with them now, and they were sorry for him in his loneliness. Perhaps he knew it and it was that which made him hate them at times, he was very proud. Always afterwards I was haunted by the thought of that sensual dreamer, solitary in his bare house and his Naturphilosophie, while around him throbbed the pulse of the real earth swelling with increase, worshipping fertility.

Nicolaie Dumitrescu, now that work on his own land was almost done, turned his activities in another direction. He was headman of the village and his responsibilities were heavy. Or so he told me; I never saw any signs of their weighing on him. However, headman he was for a year and he must attend to his duties. The bridge over the river was in very bad repair and the heavy carts, laden with the harvest, had further weakened it. But there was not enough timber to rebuild it belonging to the village, so he would have to ride over the hills to Jiblea, where the Government forestry agent lived. Would I go with him? I said that I would.

It was on the evening before his proposed journey that he made the suggestion. The next morning he said we must delay our departure as he had forgotten that it was the day of Nicu Popa's pomană and I ought not to miss it. I noticed that Nicolaie, if ever he wanted to enjoy himself, made me the excuse. As there was a remarkable number of events or days that had to be celebrated, this happened frequently.

A pomană is a survival of the Roman custom of feasting the dead. I appreciated it more later when I attended a funeral in a Transylvanian village where the rites throughout were Roman. It is a feast at which the food and drink consumed are intended to support the dead man on his journey to the next world. Three pomană are held, the first on returning from the funeral, the second after eight days, and the third, as a rule, at the end of six weeks.

Nicu Popa's pomană was the third. It was overdue; but ever since his father's death two months before he had been very busy. What with rebuilding his father's house, which was almost falling down, and getting in the neglected crops he had neither had the time nor the money to give a pomană. Now the house, though not completed, was at least weatherproof, the corn was safely housed, and kinsmen were helping to provide food.

Nicu was twenty. I did not know him well then, though later we were to have great times together. He was not tall, but strongly built, quick, athletic in his movements, delighting in feats of strength. His black hair was brushed back from his high forehead, his brown eyes though lively could look very soulful when he spoke of what moved him; love moved him often. He had a large mouth and perfect teeth. His mother had separated from his father and returned to live in the village in Transylvania, across the Carpathians, where she had been born; his younger brother lived there with her. Nicu was better educated than most peasants, for he had been to school in Sibiiu. He had a smattering of German and Hungarian and had read Oscar Wilde. But I think the pleasure that he got from his education was more in the fact that he had learned and read certain rather difficult things than in any real appreciation of them. What genuinely appealed to him were the poems and songs on his own people. Those he understood and loved, and when he spoke of them his voice sang.

He lived at the far end of the village nearest the mountains, beyond a broad, dry bed of a torrent. Not many trees grew there, for in the spring the water came rushing down from the hills bringing with it rubble and stones. But in place of the green of trees it had the rich earth-colouring shaded and transformed by the different soils carried on the floods. So that when I went that way in the evening I was reminded of the exquisite deserts of New Mexico, the setting sun intensifying the colour and painting the walls of the mud-plastered houses with a fiery glow.

When Nicolaie and I came to the house about midday the pomană, so far as the less important friends of the dead man were concerned, was in full swing. About a hundred of them were in the yard eating their heads off at a long table made from planks laid on upturned boxes. Behind them women were preparing food in great pots and serving it as fast as the diners could swallow. Fat cakes of mamaliga as large as footballs were being distributed, for mamaliga packs down well in the stomach and does not leave too much room to be filled with more interesting dishes. There was no music, but otherwise everything was going with a swing, with much chatter and laughter and clinking of glasses.

Nicu, perspiring and important, asked us if we would wait a little as the priest was coming and we would eat in the one room in the house which was almost habitable. About one o'clock he came, an insignificant, little man with a straggly beard, large, watery eyes, and the pale, silky skin common to many priests of the Greek Orthodox Church. His manner was effeminate and he spoke mincingly with an air of great knowledge. I had never seen him before, but it was only then that it struck me as strange that I should not have done. I learned afterwards that he had married a woman with plenty of money, lived in a brick-built house outside the village, and considered himself rather above the duties of a village priest, although in fact he was quite an ignorant person. It was rumoured that he had a bathroom.

Meanwhile Nicu's more intimate friends and relations had arrived. Brătianu, the butcher, a loose-limbed giant with immense, red hands, was a cousin. I had often passed his shop down by the river. It consisted of two willows from whose branches hung chunks of meat and sometimes a side of pork. Then there were the brothers Grigorescu, the village bakers, handsome, study men with clipped, black moustaches and glowing smiles. One of them, Anton, had married Nicu's sister, a teasing creature with daring eyes. The bride's father from Moraştio was there, a friend of old Popa the dead man. Maria came too with a group of women.

We went into the little room. But for the table and benches it was bare. It had been cleaned and whitewashed, but the glass had not yet been put in the windows which looked over the feasters in the yard. The priest took his place at the head of the table and the men with him; the women sat all together at the lower end.

The dead traveller was certainly well nourished on his journey. After baiting our appetites with a great deal of olives and ţuica, we waded into soup filled with chunks of meat and vegetables; there followed in turn, highly flavoured rissoles, mamaliga, fried chicken, and cabbage. It was all washed down with new wine which looked and tasted like pink ginger-beer. It was lucky that the deceased, being a Romanian, was impervious to indigestion.

As every one became increasingly cheerful it was clear that little respect was felt for the priest. He was there only because it was the custom to have a priest at a pomană. But their jokes were directed not only at him but at the religion he represented. It was all done in good part and the foolish little priest took it very well, though at times he had to uphold the dignity of his cloth by an upraised finger or a pursed mouth.

"Ah, parinte, your prayers did not bring rain when we needed it. How was that? Sunday after Sunday, and still no rain."

"Neither did your paparuda, irreverent man."

"But you believe in the paparuda," laughed Brătianu, "I saw you watching for rain afterwards. You were disappointed, eh?"

"They are making fun of the priest; it is not fair," said a woman at the other end of the table. "Take no notice of them, domnule," she called to him. "They are wicked men. Nicolaie Dumitrescu has a devil him; my husband has seen his horns."

There was a roar of laughter at Nicolaie's expense, and the priest with a weak smile raised two fingers in admonition. Then turning to me he asked me about the Church in England, inquiring the English equivalents of his religious terms. He seemed to get a lot of satisfaction out of the information, jotting down odd words like "God," "church," "altar," "prayer," and so on.

At the end, before the priest rose to make the customary prayer, the funeral cake, the coliva, was brought in and a lighted candle set on it. Rising, we all stretched our hands out to the plate on which it stood and lifted it from the table. Then the priest began to intone. The prayer seemed endless, and one by one the feasters dropped their hands from the plate and straightened themselves till I felt sure the cake would fall. But at last with a final chant the ceremony was over, and we sat down to partake of this last food in honour of the dead. The cake was made simply of corn, nuts, and honey and tasted damp and mawkish.

The pomană was over, but work had been interrupted for the day. The men strolled around the house commenting on the workmanship, the women stood in groups gossiping, loth to return to their housework. As Nicolaie and I walked back up the road in the heat of the afternoon I suggested to him that we ought to start soon on our journey; Jiblea was twenty miles away. He smiled lazily.

"A dead man can travel on a pomană. But I cannot. I have eaten too much. I must sleep."

There was clearly no moving him. When we reached the house he lay down and immediately fell fast asleep. As I had no idea what kind of a journey was before me I did the same.

About half-past four we started and I soon resigned myself to an uncomfortable ride. My horse, like most peasant horses, appeared to have no interest in life besides irritating its rider. When it walked it went so slowly that I had to goad it constantly, whereupon it would break suddenly into a stumbling, short-paced trot that was more than hard on my overloaded stomach. Only when it cantered did it move with any semblance of athleticism, but as the road led always either up or down long, steep hills this did not happen very often. The saddle was made of wood and the stirrupleathers were much too short for my long legs and could not be lengthened.

There were innumerable delays. Nicolaie stopped to talk to nearly every one he met, and at one point his horse cast a shoe. My consolation was the country through which we passed. For a while we rode up and down a succession of low hills, sometimes entering beech-woods where the leaves were at last beginning to change colour. Then after a long climb I saw from the summit of a hill the full sweep of the Carpathians. Nicolaie halted.

"You see the high, jagged peak," he said, pointing to the north-west. "In the gap below there is Jiblea. It is late, we must hurry."

He set off at a scrambling trot down the rough hillside.

All things were now lighted with the clarity of evening. A narrow plain lay all along the foot of the mountains, and from where we had halted a succession of hills rolled decliningly till they merged in it. The air was so still that all movement seemed suspended; there was that feeling of desirable but unreal perfection that is in the landscapes of Italian Primitives. Away on the lower slopes beyond the plain were white villages surrounded by the cloudy green of vineyards. The earth of the stripped cornfields glowed red.

Just as the light was going we came to the plain and crossed a broad, dry river-wash. Beyond, surrounded by pine-woods black against the paling sky, stood a ruined monastery. We dismounted and led our horses through the gateway. Hearing our approach a monk emerged from a little hut in the courtyard. I went into the chapel with him. It was so dark in there that all I could distinguish of the frescoes which covered the walls and roof were the pale faces of the rapidly decaying saints. In the thick wall of the apse was a ragged hole made by a German shell. The monk told me that the monastery was two hundred and fifty years old; since its desertion thirty years before he had lived on alone in the hut. The cloisters were crumbling and in many places the roof had fallen in. Was he at all lonely? No. He was quite content to serve the Lord in a place that had once been dedicated to Him.

We went on, urging our horses into a canter over the plain. But it was dark when we reached Jiblea. We found the forestry agent in his office and the business of the day started. I thought it would never end. Just when some conclusion seemed to have been reached the discussion would branch out again in another direction; interchange of gossip did not hasten matters. At last it was arranged that the agent would meet Nicolaie in the Government forests above the village and point out the timber that could be used for the village bridge.

Then these two decided to show me the town. As it was pitch-dark and there were few lamps it seemed rather pointless. But out of politeness I submitted. Jiblea is on the left bank of the river Olt and is a drab place with nothing of interest in it. So we crossed the river into Călimaneşti, an offspring of the older town and a kind of health resort with mineral waters. The two biggest up-todate hotels were empty, and the whole place had that sourly melancholy atmosphere which all such places have in the off-season. Seeing a cat with tail erect walking beneath a lamp I thought that that animal of all living creatures was the only one which could retain its dignity in any circumstances, however reduced.

A very fat man with a broad-brimmed hat and a cloak flung around his shoulders stopped us. He was quite absurd and started to talk rapidly to me in French. He was a painter, a bosom friend of the agent. He had studied much in Paris; was it not a wonderful place? He had been to London too, but long, long ago. Always he came to Călimaneşti in the autumn because the colouring was so beautiful. He found the mountains hanging above the town also very simpatic. Did he climb them? No, no, he was too fat. There was an exhibition of his work in one of the hotels. He would be transferring it soon to Bucharest. Would I like to see it now? Again I submitted. His paintings were terrible.

It was now about nine o'clock and I was getting very hungry. After my twenty-mile ride I had forgotten the *pomană*, at which, having only a limited capacity, I had exercised some restraint. Nicolaie, like all Romanians, ate such an immense quantity at a time that he could forget all about hunger till the sight of a laden table reminded him. He was not hungry, he said, and anyway he was enjoying the experience of walking about this great town in such distinguished company. We were going to have supper with his brother-in-law, with whom we would spend the night.

"How far away is that?"

"Oh, only about four kilometres."

I knew something about Nicolaie's kilometres by this time and so refused to go any farther till I had eaten. We went into a restaurant, and I had a large plate of ham while the others drank țuica. Soon we were all merry. The painter became extremely mellow, and with a knowing smile on his immense and foolish face brought out a postcard photograph of himself.

"I give it to you as a keepsake. It was taken in Paris when I was eighteen." He signed heavily and sentimentally.

I thanked him extravagantly and gazed long at the picture, trying to find the likeness. It was there all right, the same moony expression, the same saucer eyes looming out of an already plump face. I longed to ask him if he had been carrying it about with him for the last thirty years as a constant reminder of the frailty of youth and beauty, or if he had heard of Narcissus.

"When my friend, the agent, comes over to your village I will come too. We will have a picnic in the woods even as when I was young. Ah, those picnics ! "

About ten o'clock Nicolaie became restless. We had better move or his brother-in-law would be asleep. Also he wanted some supper. So waving affectionate farewells we set off on the road we had come. The night was black, and the road treacherous with frequent narrow bridges without rails over deep gullies. When we had gone about four miles I asked Nicolaie if we were near the house.

"Quite near, quite near. We shall see the lights soon."

But no house appeared. Several times I asked the same question and received the same reply. I became sulky and refused to talk. Towards midnight, after riding some ten miles, we arrived. Nicolaie shouted and his brother-in-law appeared with a lamp. He did not seem in the least annoyed or surprised at being disturbed and even helped us to unsaddle our horses.

Taking us up to our bedroom he asked us what we would like for supper. His wife was in bed, but he would soon fry us something. But I was too tired to ear and meant to get my own back on Nicolaie, who was very hungry, for deluding me over the distance we had had to ride. I took off my boots and thanked him extremely for his offer but could not think of troubling him.

"It is no trouble for him," said Nicolaie plaintively.

But I was adamant. Nicolaie, who out of politeness could not eat alone, went hungry to bed. There were in fact no beds, not even a scattering of straw on the floor, but lying down as we were on the boards and wrapping ourselves in blankets we slept as soundly as the dead man we had feasted earlier in the day.

In the morning our patient host appeared with plates full of fried chicken, fat mutton, and mamaliga. I am not good at starting a day on that sort of food so Nicolaie wolfed the double share. I had a glass of water and a hunk of bread, for coffee is a rare luxury with peasants.

When we came to saddling, Nicolaie found that his horse's back had been badly chafed. So taking turns on my horse we walked slowly home, reaching the village at sundown.

The next day, when there was a return of fierce heat, we went up in a party armed with axes to meet the forestry agent. As we wandered among the silvery trunks of the great beeches, marking the trees, there came a cry from one of the men.

"A bear, a bear ! See, there he goes."

I caught a glimpse of a brown body and joined in the chase. But we soon gave it up. The crashing of its swift flight died away and the silence of the forest returned.

I do not know what kind of a picnic the painter had visualized on this expedition, but his dream must soon have been shattered had he been there, for, for once, we ate nothing all day. He had sent a message to say that the light was perfect for a view he wanted to paint and was most grieved that he could not come.

"As for that," laughed the agent, shaking the sweat off his fingers, "I do not know. But no horse would carry him on such a day as this."

CHAPTER 10

SMARANDA, THE NUN OF VALENI

◆

One morning, a few days later, Nicu Popa sent a message asking me if I would like to go to the Requiem Mass which would be held that afternoon at the nunnery of Valeni a few miles away. But I felt lazy. I knew too that there would be more celebrations of a material kind and for the moment I was tired of feasting the dead. I apologized to Nicu, who was not in the least offended and said he would show me the nunnery another time.

So on the following Sunday, Nicu, Costica, and I walked up the long hill which led to Valeni for the morning service. It was a day of warm sunshine and a sky flecked with little white puffs of cloud. In the beech-woods which were beginning to flame with the triumph of autumn the air was sour-sweet. The gentleness of summer's late sleeping pervaded the countryside. We could not hurry on such a day and the path was steep. We moved slower and slower until at last we sat down on a log. It was right to sit silent and contemplate, said Nicu. A thin haze made the valley, visible through a break in the towering multitude of silvery tree-trunks, seem infinitely remote. There was no contenuous line of earth linking us with it, for where the forest ended the ground fell away sharply. It was as though we were a part of another world dropped through the sky and hanging suspended above a strange land.

"You will not be leaving us yet?" asked Nicu.

"He will be here another month," said Costica persuasively. "Will you not?"

I had been trying for some days to make up my mind to break the news that I was going soon. It was more difficult than I had thought. Not until now did I realize how quickly I had come to love these people, and it stirred me to know that my coming had meant more to them than just a welcome distraction in the steady round of their existence. I do not think I was flattering myself in this. Their affectionate natures would have responded equally to any stranger who showed sympathy with their view of life and was ready to laugh with them rather than at them. But time was passing rapidly; I was to be home by Christmas and I had far to go and much to see.

"I shall be leaving in a week," I said.

There was silence for a moment and they both looked at me. Then they burst out, talking together.

"But you cannot go yet . . . you have been here only a little . . . there are many things to be done. . . . No, no, it is not possible. Of course you will stay; we will make you. Another week, what is that? . . . Why not go now?"

I got up, laughing.

"We are forgetting the church; we shall be late. Come."

But Costica grabbed my arm.

"Say first that you will stay. What are two weeks, three weeks in the whole of life?"

"If you go in a week," said Nicu, "I shall go with you."

"And I shall be left here. I cannot go. I have to work," broke in Costica.

"I will think about it," I said, anxious to change the subject, which seemed suddenly to have become serious. We went on and soon were talking of something else.

Some way before we reached the nunnery we could see it above us flanked by pine-woods on the summit of the hill. A high wall surrounded it and we entered the courtyard through the gateway beneath an ancient bell-tower. Within there was no air of grim asceticism. The houses of the nuns were built against the walls, low, plastered buildings of all sizes, some washed blue, some cream or white; before each was a veranda with a carved rail. The Byzantine chapel stood in the centre, and before it, in a plot of grass, grew an immense walnut-tree.

The service had been started some time when we arrived, and for a few minutes we stood in the nave filled with peasants in their fine Sunday clothes. As was customary the women were all together at the back. The mother superior, catching sight of me standing by the wall, came towards me and led me to the apse. Leaning against a choir-stall I watched, fascinated. But for Nicu and Costica, who stayed by me, there were only the nuns.. One of them was reading from the Bible in a low flute-like voice. From the rest there was no sound, no movement. The whole of the interior of the chapel was frescoed, the colours mellowed with age. But the black of the nuns was relieved only by their hands and faces. Many of them were young, and some, I thought with regret, beautiful. There was no order in their seating. They were grouped as a ballet suddenly stilled. Some crouched on the floor, others stood, leaning against the stalls. Of the rest, seated, some rested their heads back against the hard wood so that the beginning of their throats was just revealed, others had their hands laid on the arms, or, leaning forward, rested their chins on their closed fists. Yet in their very immobility there was life. With deep attention they listened to the reader, their eyes fixed on her.

In the fascination of those black-robed figures with their pale hands and faces in the painted chapel there was one who drew me again and again to look at her. She might have been any age from thirty to forty; her oval face framed in black was unlined, would have been childlike but for the shadows beneath her large, dark eyes. Her mouth drooped a little at the corners as though she wished to smile but could not, try as she might. Her features were delicate and moulded almost flawlessly. But it was her eyes that compelled me; they were the most beautiful I have ever seen, possessing an intensity which yet did not make them hard. Once, as I watched her, our gaze met for an instant and I was conscious of her seeing me only as something in the foreground of a vista infinitely deep. Then her eyelids dropped and there was only the line of her lashes black against her skin and, above, the perfect arches of her eyebrows. I felt strangely ashamed, as though I had looked into something forbidden, yet longed to catch her glance again to see if I could learn the secret that lay behind her eyes.

I regretted then that we had dallied so on the way; the service was over too soon. For the first time there came a rustle from the dark figures, the tableau came to life. The gates in the screen which hid the altar opened and an aged priest, his full beard reaching almost to his waist, his hair touching his shoulders, appeared clad in vestments of green and gold. In a deep, rich voice he uttered a short prayer; with hand upraised he gave his blessing to the cloud of blackbirds and their congregation.

Then once more we were out in the dazzling sunlight. The peasants moved off through the gateway, the nuns went to their little houses against the walls. The courtyard was deserted but for a peasant with a basket of grapes. We brought some from him and he sat down with us in the shade of the walnut-tree. A fountain splashed and ran, the sound bringing coolness of the still heat of midday.

Presently the mother superior came from the chapel and invited me to her house. She was a gracious old lady, short and square and with a ruddy face. But for all her kindly manners there was an air of stern authority about her which suggested that she could be grim enough if any one crossed her. She showed me the rolls of white cotton material which the nuns made. It was finely woven and absurdly cheap. Many of the peasants who did not weave their own bought it for their clothes. The landowners too used a good deal of it in their houses.

I asked her what distinctions there were among the nuns in their mode of living. She told me that in the houses on her side of the quadrangle lived those who spent all their time in prayer and who spoke to no one. In the other houses, which were more gaily coloured, lived those who led the ordinary life of the nunnery. But for specified periods of prayer and silence they worked at the looms or went into the villages to visit the sick.

When I left her I found Nicu and Costica waiting to show me the cemetery outside the walls. There, surrounding a tiny chapel, were scores of triple crosses, some well carved by friends or relations of the dead. High trees surrounded it and the grass grew tall and lush about the graves. Nicu said that no wind ever blew there, it was so hidden by the woods; the very place for a long sleep. Many from the village were buried there. Nicu showed me his father's grave.

We went into the crypt below the chapel. Along three sides were shelves on which were boxes each with a name and with the skull of the owner placed on the lid. Nicu and Costica became very interested.

"Ah, here is Josef Koveindl. You remember him?"

"And Grigorie Ursian is over here. He was a strange man."

"I did not like him." Costica halted by a box. "Ioana Gusti. I wept when she died. It was very sad; she was a cousin."

All these boxes contained the bones of the departed. Apparently they were dug up after a decent interval, and, labelled, were brought into the crypt so that they could be visited by any one who wished to renew their acquaintance. On the floor were large boxes containing a jumble of bones and skulls.

"Whose are those?" I asked.

"I do not know. The caretaker has mixed them up." Nicu lifted a skull and stared at it. "I wonder. Who do you think that looks like, Costica?"

Costica laughed. "Old Stan Popescu; he had a pig's head."

So we went the round. "Do you remember old what'shis-name," and "Well, I never, here's thingummy. I'd quite forgotten him." At the end I felt that I knew them all quite well.

We returned down the hill from the nunnery by another way which led through a pine-wood. There we stayed for a while, stretched on the pricking pine-needles, breathing deeply the bitter smell of the resin drawn out by the heat.

"I think it is sad," said Costica, "that so many of the nuns are beautiful."

"I, too," answered Nicu. "What is the good of a girl being beautiful if she has no one to love her? She will fade like a flower without water. If only some of them were in the village !" He sighed sentimentally.

"If they were," I said, "they might not be so beautiful to you. Up there they are because you know you cannot have them."

Costica laughed and, rolling over, kicked Nicu.

"That is so, stupid. You are always after the girls."

"Are any of them from the village? " I asked.

"There are two there now."

"Do you know who . . .?" I described as best I could the nun who had fascinated me during the service.

They thought a moment.

"That sounds like Smaranda Ionescu," said Costica. "Yes, it must be she."

"Can you tell me anything about her?"

"Surely. But I have only heard the story. I was too small to know it when it happened."

"I should like to hear."

Costica wrinkled his eyes in the sunlight.

"You have seen how she is now. When she was younger she was very beautiful. Her father was proud of her and spoiled her. He would not let her work in the fields; he was afraid the sun would burn her skin. The people used to say she was ' like a blade of corn among weeds, like a peacock among the birds.'"

"But," put in Nicu, "I have heard that though she was beautiful she used to go down alone to the river like the other girls at Easter and pray. You know the prayer: ' From the great lords and ladies, from the goats and the ewes, even from the little birds and the stars let love be taken and given to me.'"

Costica took up the thread. "All the young men in the village were in love with her. But she went from one to another till nearly all of them had asked her to marry. She liked to be in love, but she did not want to marry. The young men became angry; even her father said he would beat her. But she was like a bird, she did not care. People said she was crazy. Then, when she was about twenty years old, her father became ill and asked a kinsman in another village if he could send a man to help with the harvest. Her cousin Petre Bucuţa came. She fell in love with him. Petre had heard about the other men and would not speak to her, until one day-"

"It was by the river," said Nicu - their voices ran one into the other so easily that I hardly noticed the break - "she was washing clothes and

---

[1] Pronounced Bucutsa

her neck was smooth in the sunlight as she bent over her work." He paused, as though a memory had stirred him. "Petre kissed her."

"Every one was surprised," continued Costica, "when they heard that Smaranda and Petre would be married after the harvest. But when Petre was away to tell his father the war came and he had to go to fight. He was killed before he could return. When the Germans came to help the Magyars nearly all the people left the village and went over into Moldavia. There was a big camp there of refugees. Smaranda went too, and in the spring she had a son. My mother was with her, and she has told me that Smaranda was not very unhappy. She was strange after she had been ill and said that her son was Petre born again. But in the winter typhus came and her son died. Smaranda looked after the sick and hoped she would die too. When the war ended she walked back with the others who had been left from the village. But when they came to where they could see the houses and the fields they knew she stopped. She said that the Lord had taken Petre and her son, so she would give herself to the Lord. The others wanted to get to their homes, so they did not argue with her." Costica turned on his side, looking back up the hill. "That is all. Now, though the girls in the village still go down to the river at Easter to ask for the beauty of the stars, Smaranda is at Valeni. ' as the white cherry-tree of the mountain, flowering in the forest.'"

"Which shows," added Nicu, crossing himself anxiously, "that perhaps the Lord can make mistakes."

CHAPTER 11

THE ANCIENT CAPITAL

◆

For days now the village had been filled with the sound of shuffling and pattering. The flocks were returning from their summer pasturage on the mountains. One of the shepherds said that he had seen the first wolves of winter. It was cold too up there. The frosts had started, it was time to return to the sheep-folds of the plains. Clouds of dust hung above the flocks. Hardly had the air cleared when another cloud appeared at the end of the village street. The roadway was dotted with a million little hoof-marks, as though a heavy shower had fallen without any trace of wetness.

In the midst of each sea of white trudged a donkey laden with the shepherd's few belongings and his tent. There was no straying by the way, the sheep-dogs saw to that, the tired sheep went steadily on like an army in orderly retreat. There were many bloody fights between the guardians of the flocks and the village dogs. Both were savage, but the sheep-dogs were fierce as the wolves and nearly always won their battles. They were lean mongrels with grey, lank hair and long jaws which snapped like iron traps. After two encounters Nicolaie Dumitrescu's yellow bitch licked her wounds and did her barking from behind the slatted fence.

All the flocks were larger than when they had gone up in the spring, but not so large as they should have been. The shepherds called out their troubles as they passed down the road, exchanging a few words with the villagers, but never stopping to gossip.

"Heh, Josef ! You have not so many as last year."

"No. I lost a score. The drought has been bad. The grass was poor, the hills were dried up."

On they trudged, their sheepskin caps tilted at an angle, their pipes tucked in their belts, long staffs in their hands. Through the village they did not play, glad to talk with whom they could after the silence of the mountains. When it was wet, for the rain fell heavily now at times, they wore their cojoc, their heavy sheepskin cloaks, flung around their shoulders, the water dripping from the long wool. Those cojoc have not changed in shape since the Dacian shepherds wore them in their winter struggles with the Romans.

At night I sometimes woke to hear the flocks passing. Then in the silence I heard too the shepherds piping slow tunes and melancholy, the music filled with the beauty of long months of solitude.

One day, out of curiosity to know what kind of men these were to spend their years with hardly any communication with their fellows, alone on the river plains in the winter and in the high places all the summer, I joined a shepherd and walked with him a mile or two. I did not wish him to think I did so with a purpose and pretended that I was going his way. He accepted my company with composure. He did not alter his pace, and after the first greeting was silent till I addressed him again. His eyes, though wideawake, had a haziness about them that comes from looking over great distances.

"It has been very hot up there?"

"Yes. The sheep suffered much."

"Did you lose many? "

"Not very many. But it was hard for the late lambs. The ewes had not the moisture."

We walked again in silence.

"Do you ever feel lonely when you are up there?"

"Lonely? " The shepherd's weather-worn face twitched in a smile of astonishment, almost in derision at my apparent ignorance. Perhaps no one had ever asked him the question before. "No, I do not feel lonely."

He looked me full in the face for the first time. He was tall and his eyes were on a level with mine. I felt that I had asked a stupid question. But I persisted.

"What do you do?"

"I must watch that the sheep do not become sick. If they do I cure them when I can. Then there are the lambs to care for. I play my pipe and sing and listen to the birds. There are many birds on the mountains. They sing better than they do here, it is not so hot."

I asked him if he was married.

"I have been married but my wife has left me. All the long summers I was away from her. She was alone too much. I do not blame her. She went away with another man while I was in the mountains. He was a great talker. I did not talk to her much. I do not know for certain why." He hesitated as though the sudden flow of words surprised him. "When I was alone I did not talk, so I had a custom of silence. I used to think of her much, but

I also thought of other things. Women like talk. I can understand how it was."

I left him at a path which led across the fields. He slowed his pace for a moment and took my hand.

"La revedere," he said and went on.

That is their parting in that country, rarely "Adio." They always hope for another meeting.

I watched his tall figure trudging among the sheep and the donkey swaying with its heavy load till both were hidden by the cloud of dust.

I was going to leave in a few days. I was beginning to feel restless. The heat and pleasant companionship had lulled me to contentment. When I had been working my physical state had blended me with everything around me.

The harvesting had a purpose whose end I should see, the curăţat, the culmination of the year. Now it was different. The work had slackened, people talked of the winter, how they would pass it, what the spring would bring. I should see none of this and I felt detached again. For a space I had indeed had a part in the life of the village. But there was no continuity and no fulfilment in store for me. I think the peasants understood this when I told them. They were sorry too, but their lives ran in a perfectly blended circle. I had travelled an arc of it, and with the knowledge that I could never complete it was ready to fly off at a tangent.

Nicu had held to his suggestion that he could come with me when I left, and we were now full of plans. We would go to stay with his mother for a while the other side of the mountains in Transylvania, in Ardeal, the land of hills. There were two ways we could take, the mountain road which was straight on through the village, and steep climbing for most of the way, or the road which went first westward to Călimaneşti, where I had been with Nicolaie, and then north through the valley of the Olt, following up the river. Nicu thought the valley road would be best, there would be more chance of finding places to stay the nights than on the mountains, and the valley was very beautiful.

Coming home one evening about a week before we were due to leave I found Filofteia limping about the yard with a rag tied round her foot. She told me that she had stepped on a hayfork earlier in the day so I at once asked to see the wound. I had a small medicine-chest with me which I opened, to her immense delight; she would not let me touch her till she had called the whole family to watch. Her foot was a horrid sight and was already much swollen and discoloured. I am sure too that it had forgotten the feel of water; washing it had no apparent effect, and even when I painted it with iodine I could hardly see any difference in colour. A more intelligent thought striking me, I persuaded Maria to fetch me some hot water and made a fomentation. I told Filofteia to show me her foot in the morning. She came then, holding the bandage proudly in her hand, having walked barefoot across the filthy yard. Every effort I made after that to keep her foot clean was abortive. The medicine I used was enough, what was a little dirt to that? So she thought, and so did the rest of her family who were enormously impressed by the whole affair. The fact that her horrid wound had healed before I left was attributed to my skill, though I am quite sure I had nothing to do with it. I was *domnule doctor* after that, and before I escaped I was already starting a clinic. Not that any one was really ill. But every one thought it was fun. For me who hardly knew how many aspirins to take for a headache it was a little embarrassing. I suppose Filofteia's recovery was due to the fine, natural health which she and all of her race possess. Hygiene and myself were not responsible.

When I went to call on the doctor to say good-bye, he said I surely was not going before I had seen Argeş; it had been the ancient capital of Wallachia and possessed many things I ought to see. He would lend me his car to go there. As my short stay with Octavian Fotina, when I had first arrived, had provided me only with a large meal and a sleep there I agreed. The doctor was busy with his ţuica-making, so he said he would send with me the peasant he paid to look after his car. Nicu wanted a strap for his rucksack and I asked if he could come too.

The next day we set off. Argeş was only twenty miles away, but the car was deplorable, the road, as I remembered from my first journey, little more than a track across country, and the driver drove as though he had bullocks under the bonnet. We arrived after a couple of hours, during which a number of inexplicable things went wrong with the engine. Fortunately they usually went wrong in a village where Nicu and I could refresh ourselves with ţuica. The driver, though, was always too busy sucking petrol through the vacuum tank to have a thirst for anything else.

Apart from its being a pleasant, rambling, little town there is nothing or architectural interest in Argeş but two churches. That half of Romania, Wallachia, of which it was once capital, has always been a peasant land so it is a market town. In the centre is a green square with many flower-beds and shady trees, from which narrow, hilly streets run with tiny shops, leatherworkers, ironmongers, grocers, and a few stores selling modern clothes and shoes.

The river Argeş from earliest times was a means of communication for the people of the south with the Dacians, the originals of the Romanian race who lived in the hill country on both sides of the Carpathians. Its name has not altered for two thousand years. The Greek merchants when they had settled along the lower Danube worked their way up the Argeş to the very heart of the mountains. Many of them did not follow its whole course but branched off up its tributary the Dâmboviţa, which, flowing from the pass of Bran between Transylvania and Wallachia, became the main trade route between the Greeks and the Dacians.

Very little is known of the thousand years which followed the withdrawal of the Romans from Dacia in A.D. 271. They were years of barbarian invasion when the hordes of central and southern Russia, always moving westward, were driven on in successive waves by the pressure farther east. Yet, at the end of that period, the shepherds were still with their flocks on the mountains in the summer, still dwelling with them all winter on the plains, while their families lived in the villages between the two, their language, costumes, and traditions undisturbed. And such is the strange vitality of this island of Latins that even the last six hundred years of constant inroads by their neighbours have not changed them.

In the early days they had no chroniclers of their own. Their neighbours called them Vlachs or Wallachs, a general term applied by Germans to Romans and Celts. So it was as Wallachia that this part of Romania appeared. In the thirteenth century the Prince Basarab made Argeş his capital. It was he who built the Biserica Domnească, the Church of the Princes, the oldest structure of brick and stone now existing in Romania.

Nicu and I left our driver to play with the car and meet his friends. He was always drunk, said Nicu, and had no eye for beauty. So we went along to the Church of the Princes without him.

Byzantine art, though an established synthesis of the Oriental with Greek and Roman elements, is readily adaptable to the characteristics of the countries which follow its principles. It is modified according to the lives of the workers and artists among whom it takes root. The Church of the Princes was an example of this. Its exterior was plain, would have been severe but for the mellow colouring of the worn bricks. It stood on a little hill in a grassy garden surrounded by a twenty-foot wall. Walnut-trees shaded the foundations of Prince Basarab's palace, which had been excavated near to the church. Before the door was a square of yellow gravel. A priest with keys dangling at his waist admitted us.

It was some moments before I could see anything. The walls and roof were covered with frescoes, dark with age, and reflected none of the light which came through the high, narrow windows. Then as my eyes became accustomed to the gloom I discovered the beauty of the thirteenthcentury frescoes. The priest assured me that they were unrestored, but I believe that they must have been retouched at some time, though skilfully. Although every church in Romania is heavily frescoed, these were the only ones that impressed me. Their composition and colouring gave a feeling of harmony and quiet to the building which was satisfying to the senses. Along with the tree of Jesse, the prophets, the tame and doubtful joys of Paradise, and the masochistic excitements of Hell, were objects of peasant dislike such as usurers and avaricious merchants, and in a dark corner an ashamed-looking man arriving late for church. A panorama of peasant ideas mingled with religion. The inscriptions were partly in Greek and partly in Slavonic.

But for the frescoes the interior was as plain as the exterior. There were no elaborately sculptured capitals; even the screen concealing the altar had little carving and was decorated only by paintings similar to the frescoes. The whole was Byzantine art reduced to its simplest form by a simple people.

The priest slide back a long stone in the floor and I found myself staring into the eye-sockets of Prince Basarab. To hear the priest speak of him was to imagine that he had died but yesterday. In that bare, silent church I felt deeply the seeming changelessness of that land. Yet it was six hundred years since the peasant-prince had left it. His purple robes decorated with fleur-de-lis had crumbled around his skeleton, a golden girdle still stood around his unfleshed waist. His crown and many jewels had been taken from him, placed in a dull museum. A glass lid covered his stone coffin. A fierce and valiant prince shorn of his splendour. There was a sour look about his grinning skull, as though he was sick of being stared at and angry that the symbols of his power had been removed.

After that dignified building, the episcopal church came as rather a shock. It was built about 1500 by Neagoe Vodă, Basarab the Fourth. It stood in the centre of a small open park, surrounded by flower-beds massed with brilliant cannas. Its garishness was enough to give nature hysterics. Though I believe that before the church was "improved" about forty years ago it must have been an interesting piece of Byzantine work. It is now, if, in your mind's eye, you can wipe off the decorations with which it is covered.

It was tall and compact, its four octagonal towers short in proportion to the height of the body of the church. The two above the west entrance were lower than the main towers and had long, narrow windows set askew breaking the angles of the walls so that the towers looked like fat sticks of barley sugar. Arcades of pilasters surrounded the upper part of the church enclosing sculptured medallions, and everywhere were arabesques. At that the building would have been little more than unusual, but its crowning horror lay in the fact that it was covered lavishly with bright blue and gilt. The dazzling, helicoid towers gave the whole an unseemly, drunken appearance.

As I gazed at it, trying for Nicu's sake not to look too upset, I heard a soft, piping sound like a sleepy bird. I asked Nicu what it could be and he laughed, pointing upwards. There, all around the arcading, were life-size birds each with a tiny whistle in its beak. As the breeze rose and fell the birds sang with it.

The interior was as garish as the exterior, for the frescoes were in crude colouring, looking as if they had just been brightened up. In the hands of an artist the conventionalized church paintings could be very beautiful, as they were in the Church of the Princes. But there are so many churches and so many hundred frescoes in every church that the painting of them is a business rather than an art, and most of the figures have no artistic merit. In the village churches the frescoes are frequently carried out by the peasants, then they can be appreciated because you feel that, however poor the execution, they are an expression of the people who live around that church and perhaps even built it with their own hands.

The style of painting in Romanian churches was laid down by the manual of the monks of Mount Athos. In the eighteenth and nineteenth centuries, even now, the frescoes are still produced under regulations made in the twelfth century. This traditional art of the icon ruled by Panselinus of Saloniki is an integral part of Romanian Orthodox Christianity. Perspective is hardly considered; the figures are all in the same plane and their bodies are seen from the front. Whatever the subject is doing, whether standing in profile or even intended to be turning his back to you, his chest is always towards you, the attitude of the head being the only key to his direction.

This church was the burial-place of the royal family and contained their tombs. It was a pity that they could not lie with the Prince Basarab in the Church of the Princes, a temple so much more representative of the people's spirit.

When I came out the gilt birds were still whistling, and looking up I saw a chaffinch perched on the head of one of those senseless things, bursting itself to drown the sound. I wondered how many times it had tried before and wished I could tell it that it was not worth its while, that while men lived they would always imitate or try to improve nature, and that it was better to ignore than to compete.

After wandering about the town and buying Nicu's strap for his rucksack we went back to the car. But there was no sign of the driver. It began to rain heavily, so we put up the hood and continued to wait. At last he appeared, immensely elated over a pair of boots he had bought. But when we had started it was clear that his elation was due more to ţuica than his new boots. The car broke down more and more frequently, and at every halt I tried to get the wheel away from him. But the petrol he sucked through the vacuum tank seemed to give him an added stimulus. I gave up the struggle and retired to the back seat with Nicu, resigned to whatever might occur. Luckily there was no traffic, for we rollicked along, swaying and pitching from side to side of the road, the driver singing at the top of his voice. A dozen times we nearly crashed into trees or overturned into the ditch but miraculously escaped.

I believe that man was the only one I saw drunk the whole time I was in the country. Considering the cheapness of ţuica in the villages that is remarkable. By my standards, which are, in alcoholic matters, average, one could get a good drink for a penny, be pretty gay for threepence, rolling drunk for sixpence, and insensible-carried-home-to-bed drunk for ninepence. I never went much past the second stage, though once or twice I came close to the third. The last I guessed at. The peasants are so accustomed to ţuica that it rarely affects them at all, I found great difficulty in keeping down the number of my drinks when I was with them. Anyway, ţuica is very pure and wholesome liquor.

Nicu, at intervals between clutching the sides of the car, sniffed the rain-cool air and called gleefully:

"Smell the autumn, it has come now, rich and full of fruit. In two days we shall be in the mountains. What fun we shall have."

That night before I went to sleep I realised, perhaps for the first time, that I had forgotten my restless, unformed desires to wander on down into the Balkans and across into Turkey. I slept with the knowledge that, without thought, I had become linked to this country till I left for home, and maybe long after.

CHAPTER 12

HUNGER AND HOLINESS

♦

We sat all together in my little room. To-morrow morning early I was leaving. Nicolaie, Maria, Costica, the children, Filofteia, and Floarea, even the baby Dorina had come to spend my last evening with me. We had had a special supper: Maria had killed a turkey, a lean and hungry bird, not ripe but correct for the occasion. All of us were sad; even my excitement at a new adventure was tempered by the knowledge of how unlikely it was that I should see any of them again.

"You will write to us," they said. "Do not forget us when you are gone. And the pictures you have taken, send them. We shall put them in this room, then we shall always remember that you have lived here."

I promised to do as they wished. The patter of rain on the windows started them once more at persuading me to stay.

"You cannot go," laughed Maria triumphantly. "The rain has come to stop you. The first day of the journey is long. You must wait till the sun shines."

I shook my head. "Whatever the weather I must go."

"It is no good," grumbled Nicolaie. "He is an Englishman. He loves water. In England it rains all the time. Even here where it is dry he washes twice a day. Water, water, water, it is too much water with him."

I was glad when the mournful gathering broke up; try as I might I could not bring an air of gaiety into the party. Nicolaie, the last to leave, I stopped at the door. During all my weeks in the village I had paid nothing for my board and lodging. When I had first arrived I had mentioned terms to him and he had put me off saying he would see how much I ate.

"You have been very hospitable," I began.

He guessed what I was going to say and turned to go.

"It is nothing."

I knew how little money he had and could not let it pass.

"But I have eaten a great deal of your food. Ask Maria, she will tell you how much I have had. I cannot take it all for nothing. It is not right."

He faced round to me with a smile. He was not a dignified man, less so I think than any peasant I knew, a foolish, garrulous person with rather pathetic eyes, a drooping moustache, and giggling laugh. I had often been irritated by his chatter. But at that moment he underwent a change. He became all at once a representative of his people, a symbol of its grace and hospitality. He ceased to be *pițigoiu*, the tom-tit; he did not even gabble his words.

"What is not right?" he said. "That I should not take money from a guest? Am I the keeper of an inn to steal money from a stranger? While you have stayed with me my house has been your house, my food your food. You have worked in my fields, you have played with my children. You are one of us. Have you not been happy with us?"

"Indeed I have."

"Then that is good, that is right. We are friends."

He clasped my hand and went out.

I stood where he left me, marvelling and a little ashamed. It would have been insulting to have spoken again. The oil in the lamp was low, soon the light would be spent. Yet I hesitated then whether I should go to bed or go out to see the village by night for the last time. The patter of rain had ceased. It was so quiet now and I wanted to gather up the preceding weeks and see them as a whole, not lose them in sleep at their very culmination. As I waited with the silence pressing against my head the door opened softly and Costica appeared.

"I was afraid you had gone to sleep. Can we talk a little?"

"Yes, but it is getting dark. The lamp will be out soon."

His face fell, then brightened.

"I know. We will walk down to the river. Only a little way."

So we went down the village street and off to the left through the plum orchards. Soon we became quite gay. We talked of all the fun we had had, of the bathing, of the fishing expeditions. We even sang and answered the owls that hooted at us from the wooded hills beyond the river. Only on our return did Costica become sentimental.

"I feel empty inside. I think it is an emptiness of soul. When I come back in the evenings with whom shall I talk? I shall open the door and there will be no one in your room. Then I shall go to the inn and I shall drink țuica, perhaps too much țuica. It will not be good."

"Oh, no, you won't," I said, laughing and patting him on the back.

"You will forget all about me in a few weeks."

"That is not true. It will never be the same."

"Never be the same." The words seemed an echo in the night. Nan'tséré, my Indian friend, had said just that when I had left New Mexico. Why do men say that at parting? It gives a bitter pleasure to the speaker and the hearer. But it is false. Those of us who are fortunate in our friends may leave some impress behind us. But it is a slight one. People come and go and life goes on just the same. Even as I knew that I was little in that Indian's lonely life so I knew that to Costica I should soon be only a memory to joke on in long, winter evenings. Life in out-of-the-way places is self-contained, the people of those communities form well-stocked lakes. A man who comes to one of them is like a wanderer who pauses to fill his cupped hands, and, drinking, goes on refreshed in mind and body, seeing new beauty in the inspiration the water gives. But only while he is troubling the waters does the lake know his presence. Then the ripples subside, the fish go about their business. Only a merman can enter into their lives. There have been, perhaps there are, a few mermen. Many have partly grown a fish's tail, but they cling to the bank with their hands.

Anyway I am sure that dear, sentimental Costica, with his love-songs, his good looks and lazy, easygoing nature, would soon find solace for my absence.

Nicu and I were going to start at six the next morning; I was to pick him up at his house. But it seemed that I had hardly slept an hour before I was awakened by loud shouts. It was still dark, and striking a match I saw that it was only three o'clock. I ran outside and found Maria in a dreadful panic; there were several men in the yard.

"My brother's house is on fire. Come to help us."

She was gone with the men before I could learn more. Dressing quickly I chased after them. Maria's brother was Brătianu, Nicu's kinsman, the butcher who lived not far from the river at the other end of the village. When we arrived the house was like a furnace. Brătianu and his family had been asleep when the fire had broken out - a log had fallen from the fire on to the floor. They had had only just time to escape before the building was ablaze. It had not been long before the wooden roof had caught and flared heaven-high. A string of peasants was passing buckets from the river and throwing water on the flames. It was too late to save the building. They might have been spitting into a volcano for all the good they did. But for two hours we fought the fire, dashing in when a chance offered to save something from the wreckage. Brătianu was like a madman, everything, all his savings, all he had in the world, was in that house. Beneath it in a cellar entered from the outside were his geese, roasted alive. At last the fire died; we stood back from the smoking pile, our eyes streaming, voices gone, faces blackened, and hands blistered.

"For ten years," croaked the giant Brătianu, "I have worked for that beautiful house. Now in a night it is gone, everything. Thanks be to God I have saved my children. But in two days I shall start to build another."

There was nothing more that I could do to help, and finding Nicu we went back together to his half-completed house. It was beginning to grow light, but we were too tired to think of starting yet.

"We will sleep a while," said Nicu. "The sun will be hot when we start, but we shall feel stronger."

So we washed and lay down on the hay in his barn and slept like logs for several hours. When I went to fetch my rucksack the house was empty, for which I was glad. I wanted no more farewells. But when I came back to Nicu, Costica was waiting with him. He said he would walk a mile or two with us. Crossing the river we climbed the hills above the village by the same road as I had once ridden with Nicolaie. As we went along I asked how Brătianu would be able to start the building of a new house if all his money was gone.

"We will find the money for him. Every one in the village will give a little, and domnul Stavrache and the doctor will too. Now that the harvest is over many will be able to help in the work, for he must have a roof before the winter comes."

At a troiţa,[1] a well with a shrine, half-way up the steep hill we stopped to drink, for our throats were still dry and sore from the smoke. Here Costica left us. For a moment he looked embarrassed, then, clasping both my hands, he embraced me warmly. With a La revedere he was off down the hill, never looking back. Shouldering our rucksacks Nicu and I went forward.

It was noon and we had done only two of the twenty-five miles to Cozia, the monastery where we intended to pass the night. At the summit of the last hill before we started on the long, rolling way to the plain we stopped by another well to eat our lunch. Nicu had brought a cold chicken which we parcelled out and I had some ewes' cheese. While we were eating a woman passed with a flat basket filled with pumpkins balanced on her head. It must have weighed a hundredweight. Though I had often seen women carrying heavy burdens on their heads I had never seen one with such a weight as this. Nicu agreed that it was wonderful.

"But," he said, "they do it all the time. I do not know how but they have always done it. Perhaps it is in their blood. There are few men who could. Yet see how slender is her neck."

We went on at a swinging pace, when the road wound widely we cut off the corners and slithered down the hillside. It was after six when we reached Călimaneşti, and the monastery was still several miles away. Nicu had never been there, but he said we could easily find it: it was up the Olt

---

[1] Pronounced troitsa

valley, to the right of the road on a flat promontory jutting out into the river.

The light was soon gone in the valley, the mountains covered with beech forests on either side of the river seemed to spread dark wings over the sky. At length after about an hour's walking the road left the river and we saw a light through the trees to the right. This could hardly be Cozia, we thought, with only one light. But as we drew near we could make out the mass of a building against the fretted darkness of the trees.

The gate in the monastery's wall was open and we entered the courtyard. The place seemed deserted, there were no lights in any of the windows of the rooms surrounding the court. There was no sound but the plash of water from somewhere in the darkness. We stumbled our way across the grass and the paths till we came to a door. There must be some one living for I could smell wood smoke. I rapped on the door, and my rap sounded like a thunderclap in the silence. But no one came. For the moment we were baffled. I was determined to sleep there, for we were now miles from any other place. We walked around the court to see if there was another way of entering the building. Feeling our way along the south side we stumbled so suddenly upon a flight of stairs that we both fell and began to laugh helplessly. The staircase was broad and shallow-stepped leading up to a corridor. It was only by nearly falling headlong back into the court over the low wall that flanked the corridor that we discovered that it was open on that side. On its other side were doors. We tiptoed along, conscious suddenly that perhaps behind those doors were sleeping monks.

Nicu caught my arm and we halted. Near us was a door beneath which showed a narrow line of light. I knocked gently and waited. I knocked again and there was a grunt. Taking it for a welcome I opened the door.

The room was long and narrow. The whole length of one wall ran a carpenter's bench. All about the room stood or lay crosses and wooden figures mingled with broken furniture and the huge wheel of a cart. The floor was deep in shavings. This I took in a glance till my gaze was fixed on a man bending over the bench. A candle in a wrought iron candlestick set its warm light on his bearded face which was in profile. It seemed as though he had not noticed us, for he never looked up. He was working with a knife on the figure of a saint. I felt bound to silence and Nicu made no sound. My gaze shifted to the monk's hands. They were the colour of parchment, slim almost to emaciation with the veins pale blue under the transparent skin. The nails were long and pointed. All at once the stillness came upon me with a tingling shock. Yet I could not take my eyes off those hands. At last I found my voice.

"Good evening, Father," I said, and stopped.

The monk straightened himself slowly, still looking away. Then, as though with an effort, he turned towards us. I have never seen so old a man. It was not only his body that was aged. It was as though an aura of immense antiquity surrounded him. His long hair and beard had once been red, now they were dirty grey in streaks. His eyes which were almost colourless looked through me as though he probed some dark infinity. What skin of his face was not covered with hair was like that of his hands, smooth as silk and glistening. When he spoke I felt as though it was Time himself who stood before me.

"What do you want?" he asked shakily.

"May we sleep here to-night, Father?"

He did not answer, but lifting the candlestick passed me as though I had not been there and went to the door. We followed him out into the corridor. He led us to one of the doors we had passed and went in.

"You may sleep here. We have no beds, for we are poor. But the straw is clean. What we have we gladly give to you."

We were desperately hungry, and though awed by the monk I had to ask him if there was any food, if only a glass of milk. Again the eyes looked through me.

"The brothers are all sleeping. I alone keep watch. At midnight there is Mass. I hope you will sleep well. If the bell wakes you, you will be welcome in the church."

From the light in his hand he lit a candle for us and left the room.

Nicu and I looked at each other with wry faces and held our bellies. The only thing to do was to go to sleep and forget our hunger till the morning. By each paillasse was a heap of blankets. I do not know when they had been last used, but they did not seem damp. The only furniture in the room was a wash-stand with a bowl and a bucket of water with a floating film of dust. We turned from it and wrapping ourselves in the blankets lay down. Almost at once we fell asleep. I was awakened at midnight by the bell. But in spite of the gift of a bed my stomach did not feel kindly towards religion. Nicu grunted inarticulate agreement and we slept again.

We were up by six. It was dull and chilly; the room felt like a well. Going out into the corridor I saw that the plashing we had heard on our arrival came from a running tap in the courtyard. I went down and refilled our bucket with clean water. When we had washed we felt better, though our hunger had not abated.

So we went once more to find the holy father. When we entered his room he was in the same attitude as we had found him the night before. I wondered if he had been so all night, or if the Devil had laid some spell upon him that drove him to an endless work upon that shapeless wood. Did he indeed chisel and chisel, only to find that the material in his hand yielded, like rubber, only momentarily to his touch? Was it his destiny to strive for all eternity to shape an icon while the Devil laughed?

But my stomach braved the awful mystery. With all the charm I could summon I asked for a little food to help us on our long journey.

"The brothers are now at prayer. Here we eat once a day, at noon."

Nicu gave a little moan.

"You see, Father, we came far and are very hungry."

"There is food here only at noon." And, although the ancient creature's voice quavered, there was a sternness in it that was unanswerable. But as though anxious to give us a more pleasurable entertainment, he said:

"You must not leave till you have seen the church."

Well, it was a famous monastery and had stood there since the fourteenth century. We should be foolish to leave without seeing it properly. It might raise our minds too to higher things. So we meekly followed his lead.

He took us first through many locked doors to a great hall which was used only when the bishop came rarely to the monastery. The scene from the windows was tremendous. The monastery was built on a cliff overhanging the swirling waters of the Olt, it seemed to spring from the very stones of the hundred-foot precipice, the river thrashing at its base. The mountains on the other side fell sheer to the water's edge, cloaked with dense forests. The clouds were low hiding the summits. The sense of isolation on that sunless morning was almost overpowering.

The church was intensely gloomy. But a fresco on the interior of the dome fascinated me. It was of God seated lightly upon a billowy, white cloud supported by cherubs who had every appearance of feeling the weight badly. Their plump arms were so clearly unequal to the task, though on their faces were brave smiles. God seemed quite unconscious of His precarious position, yet any moment He might sink through the softness of that cloud. I felt for Him, but my sympathy was a little embittered. He looked so confident and robust and I felt so thin and lean. His attitude of condescending benevolence mocked my emptiness.

With an effort at gratitude we bade farewell to the holy father. A thin drizzle began to fall as we set off up the valley.

"How far is it to a village? "I asked Nicu.

"I do not think there is a house for fifteen kilometres. We will sing and the time will pass quicker."

So we sang and for a time felt more cheerful. But I had a stomach-ache and soon Nicu sang alone. The rain grew heavier; it was not long before we were drenched to the skin. But Nicu's singing helped. It was then that I learned the words of the song I had first heard when the boat on which I had arrived had neared the Romanian shore:

> On the banks of the Danube
> Go the youths with oxen. . . .
> . . . If we wait for the waters we shall
> be carried away,
> For we have no brothers if we stay
> Nor sisters to be sorry for us.

The sad, long-drawn-out notes were in tune with the majestic gloom of the cloud-filled valley. But they did not cure my stomach-ache. There is nothing like a bad belly for blackening the mind.

After several hours we came to a fork in the road where a valley opened out to our left. Our way was straight on, but Nicu said he did not know if there was a village near that way, he was sure there was one, Brezoiu, only a short distance up the valley.

"We will feel better if we eat. You can get some rum, and rum is very good for the stomach."

Nicu was right. About two miles up the valley we came to Brezoiu, a straggling village with the immense yards of "Carpatina", one of the biggest timber companies in Romania. I should have like to inspect them; I stopped once to watch a screaming saw cut through a tree four feet in diameter as though it had been butter. But a stronger desire drove me into the inn.

I drank a great deal of rum, ate fine carp from the Olt, and felt better. Nicu did the same. When we set off again we were half drunk. To be so was the only way to forget our soaked bodies and chattering teeth. That being our condition the rest of the day left little impression on me, for we had also filled my flask with ţuica to keep us going on the road.

When in the late evening we came to Câineni we reached the far end of the village before we realized that we had arrived. The headman was very kind to us. He lent us shirts, dried our clothes, stuffed us with hot food and gave us beds. I shall not forget Câineni.

CHAPTER 13

SIBIIU

◆

The pollen of dawn was on the earth when we left the village. It was hard to believe that yesterday had been a foretaste of winter. Only now I saw that autumn had already come to the north face of the mountains. As the mist rose the ruddy beech forests were revealed flight by flight till the very summits glowed; the purple birches, their sensitive leaves quickly paled, relieved with delicacy the rich cloak. The smoke from cottages drifted in straight, lazy columns. The sun was warm, the distance blue. When a cock crowed, Nicu said:

"Listen to him; he knows it is autumn. His crow is loud at first, then it dies, then it ends loud again and long. The sound goes on and echoes. He is frightened and shouts to make himself brave."

We were in Transylvania now, or Ardeal as the Romanians have always called it. Câineni had once been the frontier village, and though inhabited only by Romanians had belonged half to Romania and half to Hungary.

The mountains fell back, widening the valley. But for the last time before it opened out to the plains south of Sibiiu it closed in to the pass of the Red Tower.

I do not know if the tower is called red because of the colour of its stones or because so much blood has been spilt on it and around it. Magyars trying to subdue the Old Kingdom, Turks rushing up from the south to crush Hungary, and Romanians struggling between two fires have all clashed there times without number. Even an Englishman has lent his hand to slaughtering in the dark pass.

It was in the seventeenth century when after years of struggle Michael the Brave had united all of what is now Romania. Inevitably he was assassinated. The inroads of neighbouring States began again. The Emperor with the double-headed eagle nominated Radu Sherban as ruler of the Principalities south of the Carpathians. John Smith, born in Lincolnshire, who had started his adventures at sixteen, had been several years on his wanderings when he came to Transylvania. He decided to give Radu a hand against his rival Simeon who had come up from Argeş into the Olt valley with an army of Moldavians, Poles and Tartars. After a battle which amounted to mutual massacre Radu was driven back to the bloody tower leaving the unfortunate Smith in the hands of the Tartars.

But Smith was an adept at escaping death. If he had not been England's first colonization of Virginia might have been a failure. For he was that famous Elizabethan, Captain John Smith, who at twenty-eight secured the charter and the colonists for the London Company which landed at Jamestown in 1607. In December of that same year occurred his most well-known adventure, when, captured by the Indians, he was condemned to death by Powhatan, the powerful Indian chief. While awaiting his sentence he had been imprisoned in the chief's house where he whiled away the time by telling the chief's daughter of twelve wonderful stories of his travels. When he was led out to execution the little girl, who was Pocahontas, flung herself on him and prayed her father to spare him. So once more he escaped and went on to explore Chesapeake Bay and penetrate into the interior. After which he explored New England, later offering to pilot the Pilgrim Fathers there, but his offer was not accepted. Like many men who live dangerously he died in his bed and was buried in St. Sepulchre's.

The river curled away and left us. Soon, far off over the plains, we saw the spire of the Cathedral of Sibiiu. But it did not seem to come any nearer. At dips in the road we lost sight of it, and always as we breasted a rise it seemed the same distance off. But the day was exhilarating, the way easy, and swinging along we hardly noticed the passage of time.

As evening fell we passed herds of buffalo meandering home from the fields. No one drove them, they went home singly or in groups like men returning from their work. The fields were dotted with them making their way to the road where they joined the procession which grew to a jostling mob as it neared a village. Occasionally one would stop to gaze around as if wondering for the first time where she was going. They had none of the dignity of oxen, but refused to acknowledge it. When I laughed rudely in their faces they threw me glances of contemptuous idiocy. They walked with eyes half-closed, their long heads thrust forward so that their curved horns lay flat against their necks. By the very moonishness of their expressions I could tell they were trying to forget their unbecoming rears, their silly, little tails dangling from lean, black buttocks covered with long, straggling hairs. The bivoliţe[1] were amusing companions. But even the peasants laugh at them and say they are the stupidest animals God ever made, though they have two qualities, strength far greater than an ox and a supply of very rich milk. They are so intensely superior in their own estimation that they can afford to sneer at their destiny of being the fools of the animal kingdom.

---

[1] Pronounced bivolitsay

94

It was long after dark when we entered Sibiiu. With the memory of the shuddering body I had carried the previous day still lingering I wanted a hot bath. So we entered the Hôtel Impăratul Romanilor, where, though eyed a little doubtfully, we were given a vast double room.

As we breakfasted in bed, grinning at one another over the sudden luxury, Nicu stretched out a hand, dark and horny, on the whiteness of the counterpane.

"I have been thinking," he said. "I have no money to stay in a room like this and it is not right for you to pay for me. Presently I shall go into the town and find another lodging to sleep in."

It was what I should have expected from him. But there was no fun in our adventure if we were not together.

"I think this place is rather silly," I said. "Anyway, we shall be here only one more night. It is not worth while moving."

Though it was not yet ten o'clock when we went down into the street the town had been awake many hours. There was a clear liveliness in the air—of purpose, of keeping appointments on time, of getting the marketing done early. The pavements and roads looked as though they had been swept and scrubbed by a thousand washerwomen. Yet the hustle was not clamorous. The old houses had stood there too long to permit disturbance of their quiet. Antiquity laid its soothing and restraining hand on the movements of the people.

At the end of the main street was a square with flowerbeds. There was a dip to the south, and above the roofs of the houses rose the mountains we had pierced. That day of rain had brought snow to the peaks and they were brilliant now in the sunshine. The air from them seemed to reach the town, cleansing it, making it immaculate.

The Saxons say it is such a town because they founded it, the Magyars because they once ruled it, and the Romanians because the air is so fine.

Sibiiu, or Hermannstadt as it was called under the Austro-Hungarian Empire, was founded in the twelfth century on the site of the Roman Cibinium. After Aurelian withdrew his legions in A.D. 271 the history of Transylvania, as of most of Romania, was for centuries a blank. The country was overrun by Goths, Huns, Avars, Petchenegs, and Slavs. When the Magyars first appeared on the scene their immigration was peasant not political. But under Stephen the Saint they became the representatives of Western civilization of which the Pope was the head; their advance was an apostolic one to close the passes against the eastern invaders. But Genghis Khan with his Turanian hordes put a stop to the great Magyar-Church project, and for a time from China to the Danube there were no western frontiers. But north of the Carpathians the Magyar conquest proceeded. The Romanians, its real inhabitants, living everywhere in small settlements, were not able to combine, and though they fought continually with the Magyars were defeated.

About a hundred years after this, Saxons were brought from the Rhine country to colonize and act as frontier guards. Some Saxons from Nuremberg founded Sibiiu. That is history. Robert Browning had a much more interesting explanation of their coming:

> And I must not omit to say
> That in Transylvania there's a tribe
> Of alien people that ascribe
> The outlandish ways and dress
> On which their neighbours lay such stress,
> To their fathers and mothers having risen
> Out of some subterranean prison
> Into which they were trepanned
> Long ago in a mighty band
> Out of Hamelin town in Brunswick land,
> But how or why, they don't understand.

The town has a population now of about thirty-three thousand; some five thousand are Magyars, the remainder is equally divided between Saxons and Romanians.

I wanted to see the museum, which contained a collection of Saxon costumes, ornaments, and metal work. It was in the Brukenthal Palace. Baron Brukenthal had been Governor of Transylvania under the Magyars from 1777-87, and it was due to him that the Saxons came out of serfdom. But when we arrived there we found that it was shut for the winter.

"We will go to the Prefect," said Nicu trustingly. "I am sure he will tell them to let you in."

Nicu was right. Not only did the Prefect give me permission to see the museum but to do anything else that I wanted to. He treated me as though I was a friend for whom he had waited for years. No, nothing was any trouble. If I was going to be long in the district and there was any place that it would be difficult for me to get to, he would assist me in any way he could. He was one of those rare men of whom I become fond on sight. He was sturdily built, and though not more than forty had white hair brushed back from a high forehead. His lips were mobile, however seriously he spoke there was always a smile somewhere in his face.

I found this gently ironic look in the faces of most of the men in authority whom I met in the country. It acted as a second voice while they were speaking, seeming to say, "You must listen because the vocal sounds I am making are very important. On the other hand, you know we're in a lovely country and the wine is good, the women beautiful, there's plenty of everything and no need to hurry. Life is excellent fun. There's nothing really to worry about." It is this apparent lack of seriousness which foreigners do not understand. Western Europeans know that a sense of humour is in most cases fatal to material success so if they possess it they try to forget the fact. Accordingly they distrust a man who does not treat officialdom and big business with deep respect. They may, it is true, have their tongue in their cheek, but they keep it there while their eyes are glued to the main chance. But most Romanians really do think it is all a game. They fall in with the play-acting of other nationalities and sometimes take it very seriously, even as children do. But they do not deceive themselves into thinking that what they are doing is vital to their existence or has high moral values. Internationally that is their greatest misfortune. Such light-mindedness is deeply shocking to us with our high codes of right and wrong, so conveniently high that we cannot always distinguish them. A sense of humour, after all, is only a sense of proportion and would go a long way to solving the world's troubles.

The Brukenthal collection was interesting. The curator, a cultured Saxon, showed us round, taking the utmost care that we should miss nothing, unlocking room after room and raising the blinds so that the greatest quantity of light would fall on everything. Several rooms were devoted to archaeological finds, dating from the earliest times known to history up to the occupation of the Romans. The picture-gallery was uninteresting to me but for three paintings, "The Man with the Blue Hat" by Jan van Eyck, "Woman Praying" by Hans Memling—she had a nice little dog who was waiting for her to stop—and a Dutch landscape by Philips de Konick.

The costumes of the old Saxon burghers were gorgeous. The contrast between the work, which I did not then realize was still done in the Saxon villages, and that of the Romanian embroidery with which I was familiar was significant. Though growing side by side they expressed more than anything else could have done the essential difference in the temperaments of the people. In Romanian embroidery there is no suggestion of culture. Though the colour harmonies and designs are faultless they are entirely natural. You feel in looking at them that the work has its source in the heart not the head. With the Saxon embroidery it is the reverse. Equally beautiful, it is more complicated in design, more grandly conceived. The Romanian is the expression of an imaginative people carried out as the senses direct. An expression of beauty that has survived centuries of struggle. The Saxon is that of a hard-headed, practical, and prosperous community which has devoted much thought to the appearance of its clothes, perhaps with the object of making them a symbol of their rather self-righteous prosperity.

When we went back to the hotel we found a message from the Prefect saying that a car would call for us at three o'clock to take us to the salt-mines of Ocna Sibiiului. Nicu was enjoying himself enormously.

"If the Prefect does more for you, I shall have to call you Sir." He rubbed his hands. "Let us think of something else. We will buy a map."

"You're a rogue, Nicu. I shall leave you behind."

"You cannot do that. If it had not been for me you would never have met the Prefect—Excellency."

The mines were about fourteen miles north of Sibiiu, and the way there was over a cultivated plain. In the village we found the notary who told us the mines were shut down but he would persuade the manager to show us round. Only from the closed offices and other buildings around the minehead was it possible to tell that there was a mine anywhere near. Among the low, rounded hillocks with here and there a pool we came upon the first Roman workings. The Romans had attacked the salt from the surface, leaving deep depressions now filled with briny water.

Going into a little shed we were given white coats and skull-caps. The manager lifted a trap-door in the floor and there was the entrance to the mine. With candles in our hands we followed him down. The shaft was only about four feet in diameter, and the steps cut in the salt were slippery. The walls were shiny black. In one place water had seeped in and for about thirty feet the salt had crystallized making the shaft clear white.

Two hundred feet below ground we entered a gallery. The candlelight showed nothing but the salt wall on the right. I sensed that we must be in a vast hall, for when Nicu turned to speak to me his voice echoed away and away till it was lost in seeming infinity. At the end of the gallery was another staircase. Another hundred feet down and we stood on the floor of the mine. The walls were salt and the ground was salt, the void in which we stood had salted the food of millions. Of the roof we could see nothing. We might have been standing on the floor of the world endless years hence when all the stars have died. Everything was glassy smooth and glowed evilly black with grey streaks. It was impossible to tell how far we walked through that immense emptiness. I began by counting my steps, but soon gave up. It seemed about a quarter of a mile, it may not have been so much. At one point we stopped; our guide told us that above us the roof was cut in the shape of a bell. His voice rolled in a sonorous tocsin.

"At one time convicts were set to work this mine. Little by little their sight left them and their skins were attacked by the salt. It is not pleasant to be blind. I will show you."

He walked round us blowing out our candles, and then stepped away

"Do you know where I am?" His laugh rumbled bestially, though above ground it was comfortable enough. "Could you find your way out? I could. But if I left you now, you would wander and wander until you went mad. There would be no sounds to guide you. Listen !"

For a moment there seemed only drumming silence. Then a faint, steady drip came to my ears.

"You hear that? You would think that would guide you to the light. But no, you would come it again and again, and if you were not mad by then you would hear it as you died."

I almost forgot that the man was acting. I felt walled up. My companions must have felt the same for when our guide, having played his grim joke, lit our candles, there was a strained look on their faces which they tried to banish with nervous laughs.

When we came up into the light again the manager said that no one had yet determined how much salt there was in the mine or how far it extended. The whole of the village was certainly built on salt. From ten feet below the surface it sank for ever as far as they knew. There was enough salt there to supply the entire world. Yet the mine had been closed for two years because it was impossible to sell the salt. This was the first time that I saw in this country a reflection of the world's economic chaos. People longing to consume, people longing to supply, and an unscalable, artificial wall between them.

In the village were three large salt baths named Horia, Cloşca, and Crişan after the national heroes of those names who in 1784 raised a peasant revolt against their Magyar oppressors, demanding that the country should be ruled by its own people. The revolt was brutally crushed and the leaders broken on the wheel.

As the village where Nicu's mother lived was over twenty miles west of Sibiiu, and the way to it over the plain, we decided to take an afternoon stage as far as we could along the main road and walk the remaining distance across country. So we spent the next morning wandering about Sibiiu. The old town was built on a little hill originally surrounded by a wall a good deal of which was still standing, as was also one of the gate towers. The steep, narrow "Street of the Grape-sellers" led to the new town which had grown around the foot of the hill. It was market day and the street was lined with women standing or squatting by their grape-filled baskets. Above them the market-place was crowded with *căruţe* before which were mountains of vegetables, brilliant splashes of colour rising from the cobbles. The Saxon peasant women were easily distinguishable by their flat straw hats with immense brims, and their rather sombre clothes. For their gay costumes lay in presses for gala days and were not for everyday use like those of the Romanians. Buying some grapes from them was my first introduction to them. They were not free and easy in their bargaining; they joked little and prospered exceedingly.

The Gothic church begun by the Saxon burghers in the fourteenth century stood in a cluster of old buildings to the north of the market-place. It had taken two hundred years to build. Every time that the work had got under way some new inroad of the Turks had called off the workmen to defend their country. As a result there were two churches, one grafted on the other. It appeared that the older one had never been finished for it was now used as a religious museum, its walls hung with exquisite Turkish carpets. The new church after a period of peace was finished in 1520 and contained a lovely bronze cup-shaped font cast in the early part of the fifteenth century. The great tombs of the Saxon counts and burgomasters were magnificently ornate.

The museum of Romanian art was devoted mainly to costumes and embroidery, though there was one large room containing a collection of carved distaffs which excelled anything of the kind I had ever seen. Each room was divided into sections, each section representing a district; for every district has its own particular type of embroidery and style of dress. The inhabitants of a district can at once tell from what place a stranger has come before he has opened his mouth. In some cases the distinction is clear, in other so subtle that I was amazed at the way Nicu could stand in the middle of a room and point to the various costumes without reading their labels and tell me at once to what part of the country they belonged. Though even he was balked several times in the case of remote districts.

In general the colourings in Transylvania are more subdued than in the Old Kingdom. In a great many districts the embroidery is unrelieved black on very finely woven white cotton; this for sheer delicacy of workmanship was breath-taking.

For centuries until now the Romanians of Transylvania have lived under a foreign yoke; their costumes are an expression of mourning for their lost liberty. It is the same to a lesser extent in the Bucovina, though there—being under the Austrians rather than the Magyars—they did not suffer such oppression as did their brothers in Transylvania. Yet, whether it be joy or sorrow, it is in their nature to express it in beauty.

CHAPTER 14

THE IMMIGRANTS

◆

The road, after running straight across the plain, swerved in a wide sweep south towards the mountains before resuming its direct way westward to the Hungarian frontier over two hundred miles away. At a point where it was nearest to the mountains we left the stage and walked towards the forest-covered slopes. After about two miles we reached the village, clustered at their feet. It was much larger than my village in the Old Kingdom. We crossed a large market-place and turned down a narrow lane, cobbled and with a mountain stream running down its centre.

My first impression was one of closeness. There was none of the wide-open look worn by the houses in the Old Kingdom. The end of each house faced the road, and hiding the yard was a wall ten feet high with massive double doors beside which was a smaller door equally stout.

Nicu became excited and quickened his pace. "We are home," he cried triumphantly, as, stopping suddenly, he waved to me to go before him through the door of his mother's yard.

I had a glimpse of a narrow, sloping garden, and then, before I had time to notice much else, Nicu's mother came out of the house. Though she had no idea that he was coming and had not seen him for a very long time there was no effusion of caresses. She was clearly immensely happy to see him, but her greeting, though loving, was dignified. Kissing him on his cheeks and holding both his hands she smiled her pleasure at him. Then she turned to me and told me simply how glad she was that I had come too.

In a few moments we were sitting in her best room while Nicu poured out the story of our adventures on the way. His mother watched him proudly, every now and then turning to me with a smile. She was quite young, perhaps forty-five; a little round person with a comfortable, happy face and thick, black hair. Her immaculate cleanliness had spread around her in her house. The floor was newly scrubbed white, the gay, embroidered hangings looked as though they had been washed that morning. As we were talking her younger son, Filip, came in, a slim boy of seventeen. Seeing Nicu he gave a shout of joy and seizing his hands kissed him again and again. Then all at once he became shy and sat down in silence, his quick glance passing from one to other of us.

"But where will domnul Englez sleep, Nicu?" asked his mother.

Nicu's face fell.

"Can he not sleep here?"

"If I had only known, he could. But, you see, I have only these two beds. Nastasia Dochia, you know her, came only yesterday to borrow my other one for a rich kinsman who was visiting her. I have not even any straw."

"If you had, mama, I would sleep on it and domnul Englez could have the bed," said Nicu gallantly.

"In here with the rest of us? Perhaps; but I have none. We must consider."

"Do you think Ghiga, Candid Ghiga . . ."

"Of course, yes. But it is late. You must go at once to see. And I have given you nothing to eat yet."

She looked really distressed, but I told her we had had a huge feed in Sibiiu before we had started and were not at all hungry.

Candid's house was some way off and we stood for a long time knocking on the door before it was opened. It was dark, so I saw nothing till we had climbed a flight of stone steps and stood in the lighted house. Then I had two surprises. The house was apparently quite large, for we entered a little hall furnished not at all like a peasant's house. It had a carpet and a book-case, a table covered with a needleworked cloth, and some plush-seated chairs. Candid's wife, who let us in, was a large woman, very old, and dressed in the peasant clothes of the district which somehow looked out of place. She hugged a black shawl around her shoulders and looked curiously at me, like an aged bird, as Nicu explained the situation.

Leaving us for a moment, she fetched sheets and took us into a room monumentally furnished. Everything was on the grand scale, bed, table, washstand, and chairs. There was hardly space to move. Then she left me, and Nicu, pleased that he had found me such luxurious quarters, went too, saying he would be round in the morning. I was too sleepy to wonder much at the strangeness of the place, though I was nearly lost in the vastness of my bed which had six pillows in white linen cases with lace edges.

When I opened my door in the morning a man in his shirt-sleeves was standing in the hall as though waiting for the door to open. But directly I appeared he gave a quick snort and dashed into the room opposite. I caught only a glimpse of his face, which had something black strapped around it, covering his upper lip. He wore a straw hat.

The garden was filled with flowers, scarlet cannas, dahlias, chrysanthemums, and late roses: a wonderfully gay place in the early morning sunlight, protected by the high walls from cold winds. From there I looked back at the house. It was a strange building, one-floored, but, like its furnishings, on a grand scale. Its porch must have been built first, an immense affair approached by a flight of ten stone steps and with fat pillars of plaster, the whole completely dwarfing the house stuck onto the back of it.

Candid's wife came out and said my breakfast was ready. On the porch, basking in the sun, I ate rolls and honey and drank coffee, continuing to marvel. As I was finishing Nicu arrived, grinning.

"How have you slept?"

"Well. But this is a queer place. What is the matter with Candid Ghiga's face?" I said, telling him of the apparition I had seen.

Nicu laughed quietly.

"Sh! Nothing is the matter. He has a beautiful moustache and he wears something over it at night. He is funny. You will see. I will not tell you any more. What shall we do to-day?"

Nicu had decided to make our stay a holiday. There was not going to be any work. He at any rate was not going to offer to do any. Besides, he was genuinely keen to show me all he could. For, like nearly all the peasants, he was intelligent enough to know that their way of living was interesting to me. Always I was impressed by the people's awareness. They knew that their life, their tools, their methods of working and playing were primitive. They were not in the least ignorant of the fact that in other countries, and even in their own, there were more sophisticated people who regarded them as backward. They were even prepared to discuss this with real interest. But at that they stopped, having no desire to change their ways. From what they knew of the outside world it had as many disadvantages as advantages, as many if not more than their own. If they were happy as they were, why should they change? Why have machines to do what they enjoyed doing with their hands? Why waste their lives in factories for the sake of money, when, without money, they could get what they wanted out of their own earth and something else too which money could never buy, freedom?

I told Nicu that I felt lazy and would leave to him what we were to do with our holiday.

"Tomorrow is Sunday," he said, "and my mother has told me that there is a wedding in the Saxon village of Gârbova. Shall we go to it? I too have never seen a Saxon wedding. It is a long way, but we can go back to the main road and take a stage as far as we can and then walk."

So we decided to spend the day strolling about the village, calling on Nicu's friends, and leave early the next morning for Gârbova.

The village seemed strange to me after the one I had been used to. It had no main street but many small ones radiating from the market-place and intersected by narrow alleyways. The mountains rose straight up from it, sending little streams down the middle of many of the cobbled streets. It was very clean too. But every one lived behind high walls and closed doors; nowhere could I see into the yard of a house. Yet for all the severity of its lines it was beautiful. The walls and houses were washed blue, the roofs were dull red. All the massive doors had carving on them. Many of them, particularly the old ones, were marvels of craftsmanship; up the doorposts and over the lintels were often the figures of animals, not crudely cut but worked by the hands of masters. In all the yards were trees, fruit-trees, walnut and chestnut-trees sending their foliage high above the walls and out over the roadways.

The next morning we were up early. Gârbova was over twenty miles away, the wedding there was at noon and we had some miles to walk to it from where we left the stage. As Nicu had never been there before a friend of his came with us who knew Hans Lienz, one of the Saxon villagers.

But after all we arrived early. The people had not yet come out of the morning service so we went to call on Hans. He was a typical Saxon, of middle height, very study, with a large, ruddy face, light blue eyes, and crisp, fair hair. He wore thick, black cloth breeches and high, black boots, a white shirt open at the neck, and a black waistcoat. His hat was black, round, and low-crowned, with a broad brim. Though he was very pleasant, I somehow did not feel altogether at my ease. His hospitality did not sit comfortably on him—it was a duty not a pleasure for him to entertain a stranger, I though. Though maybe I misjudged him I felt the same with other Saxons I met later. Perhaps it was only that I never became intimate with them; I should think that they were difficult people to know well. But I have met others who agree with me and say that they are a people more easily to be respected than loved.

The relations between them and the Romanians among whom they live are amusing. They rarely quarrel, for there are no petty misunderstandings between them, being so entirely different in their natures as to be able to view one another clearly at a distance. But the Saxons, who are practical, cool Lutherans, not very imaginative, devoted to labour and anxious of the future, setting much store by solid cash and respectability, look down on the Romanians, whom they regard as shiftless, lazy people. The Romanians, on the other hand, being easygoing, and finding it difficult to dislike any one except under the utmost provocation, are inclined to laugh at their neighbours, thinking it a pity that they should be able to find so little time to enjoy all the fun there is in life.

While we were waiting about for the wedding Hans Lienz showed us the fortress. Nearly every Saxon village possesses one, and in many cases it is a part of the church, a place where all the villagers can take refuge in times of war. Most of them were built as isolated towers of strength against the Turks. Of this one there remained only the tower and the great walls; the church had crumbled away. High up on one face of the tower was the figure of a woman with six breasts. Hans said that no one knew its origin. For hundreds of years it had stood there and the reason for it had been forgotten. Inside were four stories, wooden ladders connecting them. Each one was filled with sides of bacon hanging from the rafters. Every piece had a label indicating the villager to whom it belonged. The tower was kept locked, and any one wishing to cut a piece off his bacon went to the custodian, who came along to see that he did not take a piece from some one else's store. Nicu could not get over this. He laughed about it for days afterwards. At the top of the tower was an immense bell which was run to warn the villagers of danger.

We heard the distant blaring of a brass band. The wedding procession was on its way. I asked Hans if it was going to be a big affair.

"No, quite small. The family of the bride and bridegroom are very prosperous. But there is no sense in spending money on a wedding. After the ceremony there will be some music and dancing. Later in the evening there will be supper and every one will be gay. But if it cost much it would be a waste."

When the procession reached the church the band climbed up in to the gallery and continued to play while the bride and bridegroom with the attendants took up their positions. The church was already filled. The bride had four attendants, two of them married, two unmarried. She sat with them in the front row while the ceremony began. In the chancel, on the north side of the altar, stood the bridegroom between his two best men. After the pastor had prayed, one of the best men came down into the body of the church to fetch the bride. Taking her hand he led her round behind the altar and gave her to the bridegroom, who had moved forward facing the altar before the pastor. When they had been joined and blessed, the bride was led back to her attendants, and the bridegroom stepped back into his place.

It was the most impressive, without being depressing, wedding I have ever known among sophisticated people. For there is an air of sophistication about Saxons which puts them in a different category from peasants of swifter and darker blood. Neither do they belong to us people of the West who manage to bring to the simply joining of two persons who wish to live together a sense of oppression mingled with one of arranged gaiety. There was no intoning of prayers while the audience tittered and whispered. The pastor spoke in a clear, firm voice, with just that amount of expression in it to give force and meaning to what he said. The congregation was absolutely silent, so that his words filled the church. He spoke like a human being, as much a man as the bridegroom who stood before him.

During his short address, I watched the congregation. They were handsome, clear-skinned, and clear-eyed. Nearly all of them were fair. The high foreheads of the women were accentuated by their hair being drawn tightly back and fastened at the nape of the neck. The little girls had long, golden pigtails. At the end the band struck up a lively tune and we all went outside, where the pastor, standing on the steps of the church, gave his blessing to the congregation. For that wedding alone I could have loved those people, there was something so satisfying about it.

The procession set off down the street. Immediately behind the band walked the bridegroom between his best men, dressed in knee-length, flared, white leather coats bound with black, and high boots. In their round, black hats were huge bouquets of flowers. Then came the rest of the men, wearing white leather cloaks with fur collars. After them followed the bride with her attendants. On her breast was a large gilt fibular studded with imitation precious stones. The women and children brought up the rear, all walking solemnly in ranks of three.

The older women wore plain white blouses with full sleeves gathered at the wrist. Their head-dresses were white, knotted at the side and falling over their breasts. Long skirts billowed over many petticoats. But the young women were brilliant, their skirts and blouses heavily embroidered and edged with lace. Many of them wore short waistcoats marvellously worked on the front and back, and their scarves were like stoles, embroidered richly at the ends. The married women had head-dresses of white stuff like stiffened gossamer, the virgins high, circular, black hats without brims.

I had the feeling then of being not so much in a strange country as in a strange century; for nothing of the costumes had altered since the Renaissance. But I was not looking at museum pieces; the people were too robust, too powerfully flesh and blood, moving with the same proud dignity as their ancestors and the old Saxon burghers of Sibiiu.

Even when the procession broke up and gathered round the wedding-cake in the trim house of Minthe Tomas, the bridegroom, there was no lack of poise. We drank, and we drank wine, for there is little -uica made in Ardeal, drinking to our own and every one else's health. Gently, unrefusably, wine was pressed upon us till my head swam and the rich voices of the hard-headed Saxons became blurred. The band began again vigorously, out into the yard swarmed the wedding party, and, headed by the bride and bridegroom, whirled into an old German waltz.

"Nicu," I said, "we must go. I am getting terribly drunk."

"I, too. I can scarcely see. The dancers make me dizzy."

So, after shaking hands all round for the tenth time, we stumbled our way out of the village and up to the hills, where in the shade we lay down to recover. After a little Nicu said:

"We shall never catch the stage, and I am very hungry."

"I had hoped that we should be asked to the feast."

Nicu laughed. "Perhaps they thought we should eat too much. Where is Andrei?"

"I saw him last in the village. I think he is staying. I had forgotten him."

"The people know him, he will not come. I wonder why the Prefect was not there, he is at all the weddings. Perhaps he will come later. If he had been there we should have been asked to stay. I feel so sleepy." He paused. "But that is Saxon. They are very hospitable to their own people and those they know well. But with a stranger it is different. They do not mean to be unkind. It is their way."

"What shall we do?"

"We will go on to Poiana, a very old Romanian village. It is not very far, but a steep climb up into the mountains. I know a man there and we can stay the night."

So up, up, up we went till the plains and hills of all Ardeal seemed laid out below us, far away were the Apuseni Mountains, white, billowy clouds hanging still above them.

The sun was low down when we reached Poiana, below us the earth was greying. But the village, perched like an eagle's nest on the mountain-side, caught the last rays. The rounded ledge on which it was built was perhaps three hundred yards in diameter and the little, white houses jostled one another around an open square; only a few straggled away on the steep slopes. Every village must have its open space, otherwise where would the people dance on Sundays and holidays? They were hard at it now, circling about the fiddlers.

We paused a moment to watch before we entered the village. It was the *hora* they were dancing, unusual for Ardeal, where they have their own dances, more complicated and distinct from those in the Old Kingdom. There was that classic simplicity in it that made me realize how it was that they called it *hora*, from the old Greek word for dance. There was no colour anywhere but in the green of the grass and of the trees and the ruddy light of the sunset on the baked earth. For the dancers, sensitive to every turn of the music, moving gracefully, were clad in white, embroidered only in black, the perpetual mourning of their district. No master of ballet or decor could have conceived such a scene as those magpie dancers flanked by the forest and the painted dust.

We found Nicu's friend, Filip Cazacu, with a group of older men outside the inn. He was delighted to put us up for the night. As I stood waiting while they talked a hand was laid on my arm.

"Say, are you from the States?"

I turned, astonished, hardly believing that I could have heard the peasant speak and finding difficulty at being suddenly addressed in my own tongue.

"You're surprised, eh? I heard your friend tell Cazacu you spoke English, so I guessed you might be from the States."

I had hardly time to reply that I came from England when another peasant stepped forward and wrung me warmly by the hand.

"I'm mighty pleased to meet you. You're the first stranger I've seen here that could speak English."

"But," I said, "how is it you're here?"

Nicu saw my puzzlement and laughed delightedly.

"I had kept this a secret. But I wish I could understand what you say. Let us eat first though, my belly is so empty."

Filip Cazacu was going to take us to his house. But Sima, the man who had first spoken to me, said that this was an occasion so we must sup at the inn. Two others joined us, and we sat down seven to a huge meal of pork-chops and cabbage. As we ate the men talked; Nicu and I were too hungry for more than a few words.

"This ain't the only village where there are Americans," said Sima. "It's the same most everywhere in the villages in Ardeal. You see, before the war this place were pretty hard for us. Though we were about twice as many as the Magyars we had no rights at all."

"I thought there was a Law of Nationalities which let you elect your own officials," I said.

Sima laughed. "That was just a bad joke. It didn't mean a thing. The elections were all cooked. Why, if we sent our kids to school they learned only Hungarian and were taught everything in Hungarian. Result was they didn't learn anything. That suited the Magyars; they thought they could make us stupid and forget we were Romanians."

"But you had some schools of your own, didn't you?"

"Sure we did. But the State didn't pay for them. We had to pay for them ourselves if we wanted them, and you know how much money a peasant has. Even in this village, shut away in the mountains, we used to get Magyars coming around bullying us and trying to shut the little school we'd started ourselves. In the end they did close it and we had no school at all. Any one answering back was jailed. Do you know that if a Romanian wanted to leave his village and take any kind of a job to better himself he had to change his name before he could do it. Even if he was only a railroad porter he had to have a Hungarian name."

"What about their own people?" I asked between mouthfuls.

"Well, I guess they were a little better off, though never so well as they are now. The Magyars anyway were a hundred years and more behind the times. Their idea was to have a country where a few big landowners could live like kings and have all the peasants working around like serfs. That's their idea of culture and they call us savages. Gee, it make me laugh !"

"Laugh?" I said.

"Yes," put in the other returned immigrant. "We can laugh now. But we didn't then."

"Couldn't you ever do anything about it."

The man looked at me closely. "Mister, I don't think you quite understand. You English have always been free, you don't know what it is to have some one trampling on you." He spoke more bitterly than I had ever heard a Romanian speak, for they rarely bear a grudge. "Suppose you were a Romanian and loved your country, every inch of it. And then you were told that it wasn't yours and never had been, that the children of your own body were Magyars, that to teach them their own tongue was a crime. Suppose you were told all the time that you were foreign scum when your people had been in the country before a Magyar ever came to Europe. Do anything about it? Of course we tried to. But what could we do against an army? We were watched all the time; one sign of life and we were

109

crushed. Why, even if one of the few Romanian newspapers asked for the smallest thing the editor was thrown in jail. It was hopeless. Do you think a man could live in a country like that, even if it was his own?"

"When did you leave?"

"Sima and I went together in 1906. We settled in Cleveland, Ohio. I had a good job in a drug store, and Sima was took on by a man who had a big general store. We were earning good money before we left. All the time up to the war thousands of us left Ardeal. Now we're all coming home again. Sima and I and a whole lot more joined the American Army and fought in France. At the end we came right back here."

"That was a time," laughed Sima. "We hadn't any money; our wives were carrying on for us in the States, but we weren't going back. So we walked nearly all the way. We got taken up by the police in every country we crossed, but we got home all right."

"What about your wives?"

"Oh, when we'd gotten our houses all in shape they came over."

Nicu and Filip Cazacu were listening intently, guessing the gist. Now they wanted to know what it was all about. I had finished eating and leaned back, rolling a cigarette, while the two returned immigrants repeated the conversation in Romanian. Looking at those men in their peasant dress, their faces sun-weathered and the hands horny with labour, I thought of soda-fountains, movie palaces, bathrooms and chewing-gum, high wages, sky-scrapers, and city hygiene. So I asked them how they liked leaving those things. They laughed.

"There wasn't any worry about that. We had them all right and we left them because they didn't amount to a hill of beans anyway. This is home."

A cluster of mud-built houses, lime-washed, four thousand feet up a mountain-side. In winter snow-bound, in summer sun-baked. The women weaving their clothes and helping their menfolk toiling from dawn to sunset in fields carved out of the steep slopes. Drawing life from the rich earth. No money, no man nor thing their master. Freedom.

CHAPTER 15

MARS, WICKED STAR!

◆

The days once more flowed evenly. Though I was living in richer circumstances and could find little work to do, the quiet composure of the village drew around me. I knew that I should not be staying long, yet I did not feel my impermanence.

I spent much of my time climbing the hills. Many fullbodied streams flowed down from them into the plains, and on every stream were saw and flour-mills. Few of them were different from those that must have been used hundreds of years ago. They were constructed entirely of wood. I liked to stay talking there with the peasants as they moved slowing about their work. Now and then they would pause, lift the gate that directed the stream to their driving-wheels and let the water flow swiftly by while the wheel slowed gruntingly to a standstill. Out in the sunshine we would squat on the grass and as we talked the mills farther down the stream played an irregular, thudding obbligato. Those mills were as companionable as living creatures and the peasants treated them as such. Often when I crested a hill and heard from the valley beyond the wooden music, it sounded like a deep voice singing one of those halting, sad songs of Ardeal.

One day I lost my way; there were so many hills and valleys and they looked much alike. After casting about for some time I saw below me a little mill from which came a loud rapping. Near it, across a space of close-cropped turf, was a white cottage. There was no other building in sight. Curious to know what kind of mill this could be I went down the slope to it, and, as I crossed the lawn-like field the owner came out. Though an old man only his face betrayed his age, he moved like a youth, strongly and erect. He greeted me easily, for a stranger is always a friend until he is proved otherwise. I told him I had lost my way and asked if I could see his mill. We exchanged names. He was called Iorgu Rutca.

The mill was a queer contraption and was for making oil.

"It is very pure," said Iorgu; "with salads it is the best in the world."

Set horizontally in the ground was a beam about eight feet long; four holes, some eight inches in diameter and a foot deep, were bored in it to take the seed from which the oil was to be extracted. The Romanian work for the seed meant flax; I had not known that salad oil could be obtained from it. The pounders were heavy circular beams of wood five feet long, attached to a cross-beam, each with a fin projecting at the back. Behind them was a roller driven by the millwheel, and on the roller were fins placed so that, as it revolved, they hit the fins on every other pounder driving them down into the holes and with the same movement lifting the alternate pounders ready for the next bat. As the whole was semi-enclosed the noise was deafening.

Iorgu stopped the mill and took out some of the crushed seed. It looked like oatmeal.

"Soon this will be cooked over a very hot fire and then it will be left to ferment. After . . . I will show you."

He led me up the stream to a high shed. On the ground was another block of wood with a large hole in it filled with the fermented mess. An immense pounder hung above it. As he diverted the stream on to the water-wheel the pounder fell and rose and fell thunderously, while from a tap at the bottom of the block of wood the oil dripped into a bowl.

There was something so absurd about the colossal energy of the machine producing that tiny trickle that I laughed. Iorgu laughed with me and turned off the power. When we were outside he said:

"You are far from the village. Eat with me and I will show you the way later."

I lay on the grass while he went into the house to tell his wife. Presently he returned with ewes' cheese, bread, and a flask of wine.

"So you have come from England," he said thoughtfully, squatting by my side. "Can you speak American?"

"Yes, the language is the same. Only the accent is different."

"That is a strange thing, for you are far apart. But, perhaps, no. All over Romania we talk the same. Even here where the Magyars have been for hundreds of years our language is the same as in the Old Kingdom. When I was young I travelled much, so I know."

That was true of the unity of these people under whatever rule or influence they lived. For wherever I went I found no variation in the language. Though in some places there were more Slav words than in others, there were no real dialects, whether in the Old Kingdom, Transylvania, the Bucovina, or Bessarabia, and no appreciable accent to distinguish upper and lower classes.

"Have you been in America?" went on Iorgu.

"Yes," I said, and, wondering why he was so interested in America, asked him the reason.

"I have a son there. Many years ago he went. He was young and angry at the Magyars and would not stay in Ardeal. Now I think he will return. I am getting old and do not wish the mill to die. I have told him so."

"How long has it been here?"

"My father had it and my grandfather before him; perhaps it is older still. I do not know."

"Many have gone from here to America, have they not?"

"Yes, indeed. There is a village near here, Vale . . ."

I nodded. I had been there. It was called the "*sat fără bărbat*," the village without men.

". . . When I was young that place was full and busy. All my life until the war with the Magyars more and more men left it to go to America, till lately there were only old women and a few old men. Now it is getting better; some have returned to it and there are children. It is always good where there are children."

"What does your son do?"

"He is working on a railway, something to do with machines, but I am not sure."

"If he knows about machines perhaps he will alter your mill, make it give more oil."

" You think so? I have thought of that too. It would be a pity; I should be very sorry. Iron is not good to be with. It is dead and has never lived. It has not come from a seed, grown and felt the sap rise in it. The wood of my mill has grown on these hills. Before it was cut it had dropped its seed so that more trees would grow. Iron is not like that, it cannot feel, it is cold and hard."

The mill was silent now. The sun had gone from the valley, only the high trees on the hill-tops were flamecoloured. I had eaten my fill and rose to go.

"I will come a little way with you; in two kilometres I can show you your road. It will be dark soon and you are two hours from home."

Where the valley widened and a track led to the village we parted. Looking back at Iorgu's erect striding figure I could not see the mill. But above it rose the hills, and on the hills were the children its beams had left before they were carried down to the water's edge. And when their time came those trees again would propagate, so that perhaps for ever, long after the mill had disappeared, its progeny would cover the hillsides. No, iron could never do that. It had never lived so it could never die, could never have children. Poor, sterile stuff in this pregnant land.

I was not often alone. But Nicu sometimes stayed at home. He had not seen his mother for some time and she loved to have him with her. Then his young brother, Filip, would come with me. Though we became good friends, he was always a little shy. I noticed it even when he was with Nicu or his mother. He was very sensitive. At the sound of harshness in a voice, or even if it was only Nicu joking, he would look startled, become silent and close up like an oyster. His eyes were large and gentle, his skin soft as a child's. Sometimes we would walk a long way without speaking. Then if I asked him a question about the country he became suddenly alive, speaking eagerly, his slim hands mobile and expressive.

He had been to school in Sibiiu, and being intelligent was very well educated. He had been promised a job as master in the village school after Christmas. His knowledge of history was extraordinary, particularly that of his own country, of which he seemed to know abstruse details. He had read exhaustively, his mother's house was filled with the books he had borrowed or bought with his savings, papered-covered books in Romanian, German, Hungarian, and French. He had learned Cyrillic characters so that he could read the old books that were no use to booksellers since nearly every one had forgotten the lettering. From all these he had gained a store of knowledge. His mother had said he would ruin his eyes, so he wore spectacles when he read.

Once started on a subject that interested him everything else vanished. Then suddenly he would falter, stop, and look away from me.

"I am so sorry. Perhaps you are not interested. I love my country; and when I am talking I forget myself. It is foolish."

I would beg him to go on, but he would say no more till later I found something else to talk about. One day I asked him why he felt so bitter. Surely now that Ardeal was Romanian everything was well.

"My father was killed by the Magyars."

"But you are too young to have remembered him."

"He was my father."

Then I remembered something. "I thought your father died this year in the Old Kingdom. I went to his *pomană*."

"No, that was not our father. Our father was killed in the war. Soon after, our mother married a man from the village in the Old Kingdom where you have been living. They were not happy together, and after a while my mother came back here and brought me with her. But Nicu stayed with him. Our stepfather was much older than our mother and needed help on the land. Nicu has always been very strong and could work like a man."

Filip's bitterness towards the indignities his country had suffered in the past was the more interesting when contrasted with the attitude of the older men. He was young enough only to have heard of the indignities, and men who have only heard or read of such things are often more anxious to avenge them than those who have suffered them. Perhaps too his state of mind was due to some extent to his physical inferiority. He was a healthy enough youth, but by the side of most of his sturdy countrymen he was a weakling. All his strength was spent in his learning and speculation, he had done little physical labour, had had no hard knocks.

When the peasants gathered with me in the inn in the evenings and we sat talking over our wine Filip was not there, though Nicu always came. There were several "Americans," men who had lately returned to their homes. And of those natives who had not left and were of an age to fight, some had been conscripted and fought in the Hungarian Army while others had fled over the mountains and joined the forces in the Old Kingdom. But there was never any bitterness in their talk. The bad days were over. What was the good of dwelling on them? Yes, they had had suffering, but they had borne it, and now it was past. What mattered was the land, their precious earth from which they had sprung and which had carried them through the hard times. It was fit for them to live on now, and it must be kept so. They had faith in their strength.

"Why should we fear? The land is happy. The Magyars, except the big landowners, are as contented as we are. They do not want to change. Before, they had no land of their own, now it has been taken from the landowners and given to them even as it has been to us. Those peasants are good; we are all one. No one can complain if he has his own land. Hunger makes men angry. With the earth there is no hunger."

Candid Ghiga was never absent on these evenings. He loved wine and good company. He used to pause theatrically in the doorway, utter a loud "A-ha," slap the table with a little switch he always carried and then seat himself beside me. The first time he came I thought that the "A-ha" was the prelude to a great announcement, but always afterwards I knew that it was only to say that he, Candid Ghiga, had arrived. It took some time before I could place him. Though hail-fellow-well-met with every one he looked quite different. He was of middle height and had a dancing devil-may-care walk. He wore a straw hat which he never took off even in his own house so I have no idea what his hair was like or indeed if he had any. His moustache, when it emerged from its night-case, proved to be a gorgeous affair twisted sharply up at the ends. His eyes were bright and keen, though the whites were yellowing. I suppose he was about sixty. His dress consisted always of black and white striped trousers, a black coat, a neat collar and tie and white plimsolls. They may have been all the clothes he had. He talked in a rapid, jerky manner and laughed nearly all the time. He apparently lived on a pension for something and amused himself by drinking with any one he could and getting in every one's way when they wanted to work. But nobody minded.

His bashfulness of the first morning did not return except when I tried to take his photographs when he became extremely coy. I often used to try just to tease him. But he never let me see him again with the case over his moustache, though he used to burst in on me every morning to see if I was getting up, give a loud "A-ha" and vanish.

One evening when Nicu and I had been out all day, we came into the inn hungry and thirsty and found Candid sitting disconsolately alone. He leaped to his feet and wrung our hands warmly.

"Ha, here you are, you rascals. Now then, wine, food. But wine first."

He pushed us into our chairs and ran through into the kitchen. When he came back, I said:

"What have you been doing to-day?" Knowing that he had done nothing.

"What have I been doing?" He waved a finger at me. "I have been reading." He paused importantly.

"What have you read?"

"Nothing," interrupted Nicu with a laugh.

"Oh, you devil, you," cried Candid. "Get along with you. Eat your food. I have been reading history, geography . . ."

"That is very interesting."

"Yes, yes, I have many books, a great library; you must see it. Ask me where anything is, I can tell you."

"Where is St. Helena?"

"South Atlantic. A-ha, you thought you could catch me. Devil take it, you English, you don't like the French. Napoleon . . . ha . . . a genius, but Elba, ah, and Waterloo, St. Helena, damned unhealthy. There you are, I know. Trafalgar. What a fellow you are ! Do you speak German?"

"Only a very little."

"Pity, great pity. I speak perfectly. Why? Because I, Candid Ghiga, was once a lieutenant in the Austrian Army. No ordinary soldier. A lieutenant. Ten years in Vienna. A great regiment."

"What was it?"

"The regiment of Kaiser Alexander der Erste Kaiser von Russland. Write it down. Ah, those were days. Ten years. Beautiful women, music, dancing. Candid Ghiga, 1890 to 1900."

He kissed his fingers to the air.

"But why did you give it up, if it was so good?"

Candid looked at me silently a moment, winked, slapped the table and leaned forward.

"Why? My secret. I will tell you. I married the most beautiful girl in Sibiiu, in the world. Twenty years older than I. But her father was rich. I had no money. I loved her. Now she is very old. Devil take it, what does it matter? How does it please you here? How is Candid Ghiga with you?"

"I love him."

I had just filled my mouth as Candid slapped me on the back. I choked so violently that he rushed off to fetch some more wine, which he made me drink to clear my throat.

"You devil you, you're laughing at me. I know. Holy Mother of God and all the saints I shall be sorry when you are gone."

"If you were in the Austrian Army, what happened to you in the war?"

"I was clever. Candid is clever. Only Romanian in the village who could speak German. Army? On, no. Ha ! Germans came here, knew nothing, could not find anything. But found Candid Ghiga. Made him notary of the village, look after supplies, billets. ' Cannot serve two masters.' Candid could. All comfortable. Germans happy, good homes. Then they look for young men for the army, Romanians. What is Iancu? Where is Nicolaie? Where is Gheorghe? No young men. Why? Candid does not know. Oh, no. But he had told them where the Germans were and they had escaped, flown. Over in the Old Kingdom they had joined Romanian Army. Clever. To the devil with it. What a time I had ! I got a pension for it. This wine is poor. Come to my house and we will drink. No light now, so no photograph. Ha ! You scamp, I saw you with your apparatus to-day. You thought I was blind."

Outside, Candid danced unsteadily between us, his arms linked in ours.

"Wonderful night. Astronomy, stars, I know them all. Sirius, Neptune, Mars, wicked star; but Venus. . . . Oh, devil take it . . ."

CHAPTER 16

GOLD WHICH NEVER MAKES MEN RICHER

◆

One morning a few days later Nicu came into my room almost bursting with excitement. Whatever his emotions they showed at once in his face.

"Excellency," he began.

"Nicu, what have you been up to?"

He looked innocent. "Nothing. But I must call you Excellency because the Prefect is so kind to you."

"How?"

"Last night he sent a message to my mother's brother who is headman to say that he would send a machine to-morrow so that you could see the gold-mines near Abrud, and I am going with you. It will be fun."

"I believe you have had something to do with it."

"I? What could I do?"

"A lot. We will have a wonderful time though. It is a long way."

"Yes, nearly two hundred kilometres. We shall have to sleep there and return the next day."

These gold-mines were the oldest in the country. I had heard about them several times, and how the primitive methods of the Romans, who had first worked them, were still used by the peasants. Nicu and I had talked of walking there, but our stay in the village had made us lazy and we had almost abandoned the idea. So it was exciting to think that we should see them after all.

As we went round together to his mother's house, Nicu asked if I thought we could take his brother.

"It is a great chance to go all that way in a machine. Filip may not have it again. Can we ask the Prefect?"

Although the Prefect was being inexplicably kind to me I thought it might be too much to expect him to provide transport for all my friends. So I suggested that we should take Filip and say nothing about it. I was quite sure the Prefect would have no objection at all if I told him afterwards, but he might not like to be asked for his permission.

It was still dark when I was awakened the next morning.

"The dawn is coming. We must go," cried Nicu at the window.

In a few minutes we were away. Nicu and I together in the back of the car, Filip in the front with Stefan, the same man who had taken us to the salt-mines, who was as excited as the rest of us at the prospect of two days' exploration. Just as it was growing light we broke down. For some way the car had struggled at every incline, and at a rather steeper one than usual it petered out.

While Stefan swore patiently under the bonnet I walked to the summit of the ridge we were climbing. The world was all grey, cold, and featureless. Then, as I watched for the dawn, a narrow streak of brilliant red appeared in the east and, paling, spread upward till it suffused the whole sky. Every moment the earth grew lighter, the valleys opened, the hills raised their heads from their night-sleep. I knew then why the land was called Ardeal - "has hills." They stretched before me like a billowy quilt, their summits green islands on a sea of mist. The horizon was a high, jagged line.

Nicu stood by me.

"You see, far away. Those are the Apuseni. They are very old, far older than the Carpathians. We must cross them."

The car ground up behind us and we went on. Hour after hour we dipped and rose. Again and again the car failed. There had been heavy storms a few days before and often we left the impassable road and took to the country. About midday we came to Alba Julia, once a Roman citadel. There in 1600 Michael the Brave had been crowned King of Romania, and there in 1922 King Ferdinand and Queen Maria were crowned rulers of their country, united again after more than three hundred years. A pleasant, old town, the old quarter on a hill, the new spread around its base.

After that the road became worse. As we entered the mountains it became dangerous. Chunks of it had slid clear away into ravines so that there was barely room for the car to squeeze by the cliff-face. In clearings of the forests we came upon many charcoal-burners' encampments. Far from their villages, the men live there for months at a time, coming down only when they have gained a great stock of charcoal to sell. Sometimes we met caravans of timbercutters, their travelling houses built of plaited laths perched on their loads. At every bend of the mountain track Nicu or I went ahead to see if one was approaching and if there was room for us to pass.

At about four o'clock we dropped suddenly into a valley, and found unexpectedly Abrud, an ugly little town, the more drab in contrast with the beauty of its setting. We were told there that the mine was at Roşia

Montană a few miles farther on. So we climbed out of the valley towards a high rocky hill that stood isolated, ringed with mountains. On its lower slopes was the village.

Nearly ten hours of travel over only a hundred miles made us feel as though our bones had been ground together. But it would be a good idea to find the notary at once, said Nicu, in a few hours it would be dark.

As we stood in the sloping square of the straggling village wondering where to go, a big man came out of one of the houses and strolled towards us. I asked him where was the notary. He tapped his chest.

"I am the notary."

But when I asked him if we could see the mine, he looked doubtful.

"It is a long way," he said, pointing to the rocky summit of the hill, several hundred feet about us. "You do not want to walk to it, do you?"

He must have seen our disappointment, for he smiled, his rather surly face becoming suddenly benevolent.

"All right, we will go on horseback."

He strode away and in a few minutes returned leading a string of ponies.

As soon as we were out of the village I saw that what had seemed from the valley a single peak was a jumble of several rocky hills, mounting precipitously to a perpendicular crag. There was hardly any vegetation, the trail led around smooth slopes of shale splashed with red and ochre earth. Here and there tunnels had been driven into the hillsides. In places the ground fell straight from the narrow trail into the valley. The notary waved his hand.

"All this part has been worked for a long time. I do not know how long. We cannot get much more gold here because we have not the tools, though there is plenty of it. At the top, though, it is easy. You will see."

Now and again he jumped off his horse and brought me a handful of rock in which I could see gleaming specks. After riding upwards for over an hour we reached the top of the supporting hills. Before us rose the crag, encircled like a moated castle by a deep ravine. It was some four hundred feet high, dark grey, streaked with red and pitted with caverns.

Leaving our horses, we scrambled down into the ravine. I had wondered how the ore was taken into the valley. When we came to the entrance to the workings there was a line laid from it which led to a gap in the wall of the ravine where the ground sloped more gently into the valley. Presently some peasants emerged pushing loaded trucks. The trucks were attached to a chain wound on a winch and allowed to run slowly down the line. At intervals down the mountain-side were other winches to which were in turn attached, the slack chain then being re-wound. So, in easy stages the trucks reached the valley bottom.

"Primitive, eh?" laughed the notary. "I think it is not very different from when the Romans were here two thousand years ago."

He took a candle out of his pocket and led the way into the opening in the rock. We threaded our way through the dark passage sometimes stumbling into little pools. After coming into several chambers where peasants were hacking at the face of the rock we entered an immense cavern, the centre of the mine. Through a jagged hole, high above us, I could see the sky. But the light gathered the pallor of the rocks, making even the men's faces grey. A peasant on a ladder was chipping at the wall while two others shovelled the falling pieces of rock into a basket which they emptied into a truck. The notary pointed to a black smudge on the wall.

"You see that. Sometimes they are short of dynamite here. So they build great fires; when the rock is hot, they throw cold water on it. That splits it and they can work it more easily. It is very hard."

I asked him how the gold was extracted from the ore.

"You have seen the oil mills? It is done in the same way. The ore is put in the mill and pounded and pounded under water-power till it is like powder. Then it is washed and sifted in pans."

"But surely a great deal is wasted?"

"I should think that quite a half of all the gold in the mine is lost. This mine, though it has been worked for more than two thousand years, is still one of the richest in the country. No one has ever worked it properly; it has only been scratched. Engineers have been here and have called it a mountain of gold. But there is not enough money in the country to find the capital for a company to work it. It would need a great deal, for it would not be worth while if it was not worked in a modern way. The Government knows all about it, but" - he rubbed the palm of his hand- "backsheesh, always backsheesh. Things cannot be done that way. Some day perhaps we shall have a government of honest men." His wry face belied his hopes.

"Can the peasants then come and work at any part of the mine they like?"

"Oh, no. It is all done according to a very old custom. For generations, no one knows how long, families have owned certain parts of it. They work that part, and it is handed down from father to son. Only by a decision of a council of the whole village can a man extend his workings. They do not make much money. The labour is slow and very hard, and, with all the waste, they do not get much in the end when they sell the gold to the Government."

So for centuries these grey-faced peasants have worked their treasure which never makes them richer. Neither, said the notary, do they hope to become rich. While other men set great store by the precious metal, have made it the standard of their lives, these men toil only for their bread. It is simply their traditional livelihood. Men of the earth, it is for the earth to provide nourishment. They work beneath the surface, their countrymen in other parts above. It is all the same, their lives in other ways are no different. The earth is their life, they cannot be separated from it.

As we went down the mountain-side, the last light threw the landscape into brilliant relief. The stillness of the evening arrested time, and it occurred to me that we were in some ancient volcanic formation. The golden crag was the cone, and the ring of mountains the outer wall. I called to the notary and asked him if it could be so. Drawing up his horse, he turned in his saddle.

"Before men lived that gold was thrown from the centre of the earth. Now, for as long as we can remember, we have taken what we want of it. It is worth to us what corn is to others. No more. Men are stupid who spend their whole lives fighting for to put it in a box."

The light was nearly gone when we came to the village and the air had become suddenly cold with the passing of the sun. I asked the notary if there was anywhere in the village we could spend the night. He hesitated a moment and I guessed that he was weighing in his mind whether his hospitality could rise to supplying food and beds to four men.

"An inn?" I suggested to ease his conscience.

His face brightened. "I am sorry that there is no inn in the village. I wish that I -"

"Do not trouble, please. Perhaps there is some place in Abrud."

"Surely, there is a fine inn."

I caught a glimpse of Nicu's unhappy face and nearly laughed. To the notary's obvious relief I said we would go there, and thanking him for his kindness we set off back to Abrud. But Nicu was disgusted at what he called the notary's meanness. Such a thing would never have happened in the Old Kingdom. But his brother and Stefan said that that was all very well, but having become so used to protecting themselves from the Magyars, people in Ardeal could not help being reserved, it was a habit. At which we all laughed and forgot about it.

We stopped once to watch a peasant washing out the gold from the ore he had crushed in his primitive mill. He gave me a pinch of it and said it would pay for my supper in Abrud.

It was pitchy dark before we reached the town, and there were no lights on the car. By the time we had found the inn we were shuddering with cold. It was a bare, stone building and the eating-room felt like a well. After stamping about on the flagged floor and shouting for some minutes, we realized that the proprietor had come in behind us and was standing watching us. He looked very unpleasant, and shuffling across asked what we wanted. When we told him he cheered up a little and went off in search of wood. Soon the iron stove in the middle of the room was nearly red hot, and after several glasses of rum all round we thawed.

There seemed to be nothing to eat but fried eggs. We ate about eight each and drank quantities of strong wine. The more we drank the more we sang, and the more we sang the more wine the innkeeper placed on the table. I noticed his eagerness and did not like it; he had a fat, evil face. His presence in the room gave a dankness to the air which took the life out of singing, the floor seemed dirtier, the walls more barren because of him.

"I do not like this man," said Nicu; "he is trying to make us drunk. Let us go to bed."

I was just going to call for the man to ask him the price of his rooms when Nicu laid a hand on my arm.

"Listen. I do not want you to pay much. When we came to-day we all thought that we should find some one who would give us food and beds. I feel that it is my fault. It is not right for us to cost you a lot of money. So ask him for one room. We can all sleep together and it will be cheap."

When the innkeeper heard that we wanted only one room he looked even more repellent. But shrugging his shoulders he led the way upstairs. The place was like a barracks and appeared to be quite empty. I could not think why such a huge place should ever have been built. Our room was bare but for two narrow beds and a washstand at which we took it is turn to splash, for there was no soap. Nicu turned the key in the door.

"We will sleep with our money in our pockets. I do not like towns."

Pushing the beds together we threw the sheets, which were Isabella-coloured and quite damp, on the floor. We were just taking our boots off before settling down for the night when there was a knock on the door. As I opened it a woman slipped quickly past me into the room. When I turned she was already seated on our bed, giggling and chattering. Wasn't it very uncomfortable all in one bed? There was a much nicer room, number eleven, down the passage, she would show it to one of us. Her wiles were directed at Filip, who was looking his shyest. She was coarsely good-looking and brazen; bright, round spots of colour on her face. The more we told her to go away the more insistent she became; at last she became tearful, said she was being insulted and would call the proprietor.

"Perhaps she feels lonely," suggested Stefan, who had had more wine than the rest of us.

"Don't be a fool," I said, and taking her firmly by the waist and wrist I pushed her struggling and protesting out in the passage and locked the door.

We had hardly blown out the light and got into the communal bed when steps came down the passage and there was a hammering on the door. We took no notice, so the innkeeper began to abuse us, at which we all burst out laughing. After a few more curses he went away.

"It is always the same in towns," muttered Nicu. "The people who live in them are horrible. I hate towns."

There are advantages in being packed tightly in a communal bed when it is cold and the blankets are thin. We kept each other warm and slept soundly. The windows were frosted and there was a light fall of snow on the ground when we awoke. As we had only to put on our boots and cojoc we were soon ready to start homeward. After some argument we made the surly innkeeper give us some rum and left.

Stefan had decided to take a different road, though it was longer the surface might be better. We were anxious to return to the village quickly as we had promised Nicu's mother to be back in time for supper. It was her name day, the day of St. Paraschiva, and there would be a party.

Climbing out of the valley we were soon enveloped in a dense, mountain mist. Here and there the sun pierced it like a spot-light, making brilliant islands of colour on the grey mountain-side. Once over the ridge we descended spirally into a long valley. Little, white farms dotted the slopes, the crowing of the cocks was long-drawn and arrogant. It reminded Nicu of our walk by the Olt. He pointed to the farms delightedly, they were just like those in the Old Kingdom, wide-open, unwalled, and with carved verandas.

By noon the mountains were behind us and we were in rolling country once more. Nearing the town of Deva, we passed by a high, rocky hill with a ruin on its summit. I asked Filip if he knew what it was.

"It is called the Castle of the Djinn," he said. "It was once a Roman citadel. But it was there before then, no one knows how long. There was once a great war between the djinn of the hills and the djinn of the plains. There were then many hills like that one. But one of the plain djinn, by a great stroke cut off the tops of the hills and made the country like it is now from here to the Retezat mountains. He missed that hill, and the stroke was so great that it killed him. Then all the hill djinn who were left came together and built that castle on the hill and defeated the djinn of the plains. They say that the reason why the Turks, when they came to Ardeal, could not take the castle was that it had been built by magic."

Two hours later we came to a road that led towards Hunedoara. To go there meant a delay, but none of us, though in legend we had all heard of it, had ever seen the castle. When I saw it I hardly believed in it. It was like one of Doré's castles in *Les Contes Drolatiques*. Built on a solitary rock, surrounded by a ravine two hundred feet deep, it soared slim, turreted, and tall.

From the dungeons to the highest towers we explored it. The walls at the base were nine feet thick, at the top four. The warden led us, filling our ears with legends and tales of blood. He showed us the pit filled with spikes beneath the hall where captured robbers were thrown and later devoured by the castle dogs. History knew only that the castle had been built as we saw it about 1240 on the foundations of a Roman citadel; in the courtyard lay pieces of Roman sculpture, green from the weather.

When I asked the warden to tell me the story of the castle he took us up a broad staircase to a long, narrow hall. There he pointed to the dim frescoes.

"They tell it better than I can, though if you cannot understand, I will explain a little."

So with his help I read the tale.

Toward the end of the fourteenth century Sigismond de Luxembourg, King of Hungary, held his parliament at Hunedoara. One day when he was out hunting he met a peasant girl, Elisabeta Mărgineanu, and fell passionately in love with her. Escaping from the hunt he spent days with her in the forest, and in the end asked her to marry him. When she refused he left her. But later, when she thought that she was with child, she went to Sigismond and said that she was ready to be his wife. But he had changed his mind. So she returned to her home and married a peasant, Voicu. The child was born and was called Ion Huniade. One day, when Elisabeta and Voicu and their child were in the forest, Voicu left them to find food. Elisabeta lay down under a tree and fell asleep. The child, playing with his mother's ring, dropped it, and a raven swooped down and flew away with it. When Voicu returned, the raven hopped from branch to branch mocking him. So Voicu shot it and recovered the ring. Ion Huniade when he grew up took as his arms a raven with a ring in its beak.

Ion Huniade was in fact governor of Transylvania in the fifteenth century, having the Romanian title of Voevod borne by the Magyar governors of the province. Uniting his army with those of the provinces of the Old Kingdom, Moldavia and Wallachia, he spent his whole life fighting the Turks. When Sigismond's successor, Vladislav, was killed at the battle of Varna in 1444, Huniade became Regent of all Hungary. He was a tremendous fighter, a hero of whom many songs are still sung, and among the Magyars there was no one strong enough to lead them against the Turks. But the nobles hated him because of his Romanian origin, for it is not clear whether Elisabeta's child was really Sigismond's or whether its father was Voicu. This "White Knight of the Romanians" as he was then called, had two sons who in turn became kings of Hungary. Hungarians now say that he was Hungarian. But I cannot see that it matters in the least who he was, he was a brave man.

In the great hall, its roof hung with festoons of bats, were frescoes of the great Romanians of Transylvania, men who while Hungary was crushed and Buda a *pashalik* kept their independence. Chief among them was Mihai Viteazu (Michael the Brave), who has become a very symbol of unity to all men who have sprung from the Romanian earth under whatever rule they may once have lived. And to me it seemed an answer to those who point derisively to the lack of culture in these people who endured five hundred years of constant struggle with the Asiatic invaders that the boasted civilization of the West might grow.

The sun was gone and the hills were dark and velvety when we reached the village. Stefan was for leaving us and going on to Sibiiu. But Nicu's mother told him that he must stay for her party. We had stopped on the way at a house where the peasant had let us pick all the flowers we needed. We gave them to her now—roses, cannas, and huge bunches of Michaelmas daisies. Paraschiva's house must be bright for her name day. While she was busy in the outhouse preparing the food we decorated her room.

Nicu and Stefan went off to fetch wine, Filip into the orchard to shut up the fowl. Feeling rather tired I sat down. The quiet happiness of the room grew around me and I closed my eyes. Paraschiva came in.

"You are tired," she said. "I have disturbed you."

"No. I am content. I love your house; whenever I come here I feel happy."

She smiled. "I am glad. It has grown old with my family."

"How old is it?"

"Perhaps nearly three hundred years; I am not sure. There are many old houses in this village."

"Are they all as beautiful as this?"

"Many are more so. But why do you call this beautiful? You have seen so many places."

It was hard to tell her why it seemed so to me. The room was lime-washed and low-ceilinged with many beams. The wooden bed was decorated with patterns in red and blue, the pillows were in their day-cases of embroidered linen. On a long shelf was a row of jugs, the pigment on the pottery mellowed with age. A pole ran the length of one wall from which were hung like tapestries long strips of woven hemp of equal size, their ends embroidered in deep red and blue. There was a painted chest, which I knew was filled with Filip's books, and a wrought iron lamp above it. I could only tell her that it was the colour that was harmonious. I rounded my hands to show her that I felt it to be complete, that it had a strength and composure that had resisted the invasion of what was trivial. I think she understood.

"I like those pieces of embroidered hemp," I said. "They are old, are they not?"

I had seen some like them in glass cases in the museum at Sibiiu, and had been amazed when I had first arrived to find here in this cottage about a dozen of them on the wall.

"Which one do you like best?" she asked, moving towards them.

I stood by her and examined them closely. Though all were different in pattern the difference was very slight. When I laughed and said I like them all she took one down and placed it in my hands.

"It is yours."

"No, please," I said. "You are very kind. It is too valuable for you to give away."

I was embarrassed. I knew that such things could not be bought in a shop, and that if they could be I had not the money to buy one. But she read my thoughts.

"It has no price. You are very fond of Nicu. He loves you, you are his good friend. So you are mine. This was made by my great-great-great-great-grandmother. You have there a part of my family and cannot forget us." She gave a cry. "Oh, I have forgotten the chicken. I must go." And she left me with the cloth in my hand.

We sat down eight to supper; Paraschiva had invited a cousin with his wife and another man. The stuffed chicken for all its neglect was good, so were the pancakes and the wine. So was everything. We were very gay.

"I am ignorant," I said, when we had drunk Paraschiva's health. "Who was St. Paraschiva?"

"Oh, she was a very old saint. I do not know what she did," said Nicu.

"She died near Istanbul."

"No, in Greece," contradicted Filip.

"It is all the same. She was very holy."

"Her bones are at Iaşi[1] in Moldavia," said the cousin. "People pray to her for rain. But it is foolish."

We all laughed. For of course it was silly. Who wants rain in the autumn? The spring is the time for that.

There was silence for a moment and Filip went to the chest. We had begun to talk again when the first notes of his pipe, slow and long, made us pause. It was always the same. At the music, at the song which was the colour of their living, there was silence. The listeners heard in it the voice of one of themselves who - more interpretive that they - expressed the emotions that they felt but could not always tell, till at last, the music stirring them, they sang too all that was in their hears.

As Filip ended, Nicu linked the last notes to himself and began first to hum then to sing as Filip took up the tune.

> Doina, doina, sweet song,
> At the sound of your music I stay.
> Doina, doina, song of fire,
> At your trembling notes I am still.
> When the spring wind blows
> I mimic the flowers
> And the song of the nightingale,
> And when the stormy winter comes
> Your song is warm by the fire.
>
> So the days will caress me,
> The days and the nights,
> While the leaves in the woods sing bravely.
> But when they fall in the valleys and streams
> My doina is filled with sadness.
> Doina I sing, doina I whisper,
> Doina is my life.
> Doina I speak, doina I sigh,
> Without it I should die.

So they sang on the doina of Ardeal, those songs born of their captivity which had carried them through the years of oppression, telling only of the beauty of the trees, of the earth, of the spring flowers, and the bounty

---

[1] Pronounced Yash.

of rain. With such songs they could not perish, for they were the very voice of the soil from which the singers sprang. On the mountainsides the shepherds sang them and did not know loneliness.

"Cousin Ion," said Paraschiva, "do you remember 'Poor strange land'?"

"Surely I do. When my father sang it my mother used to weep. For you know she was from the Old Kingdom and was sad that there was no freedom in her husband's land of Ardeal."

He drank and looking into the empty glass began again in his deep, slow voice:

> Oh, poor, strange land,
> How long have I kept watch with you !
> I have had too much of strangers
> As the grass has of old bullocks.
> I am preyed upon by foes
> As the grass is by fresh cattle.
> Oh, I am tired of cruelty
> As the grass is of milch cows.
>
> I am as worn out with worry
> As the grass by hungry sheep,
> I have wandered all the country
> Fortune always passes by.
> Wherever now my feet may guide me
> I can never find repose,
> It matters not how far I wander,
> Peace can never rest my head.

"And do they sing that song now that they are free?" I asked.

"They will sing it always. Though it is sad it is beautiful. For there is beauty in sadness, domnule Englez, even as there is sadness in beauty."

CHAPTER 17

THE PRIESTLY EPICURE

◆

We sat on a hillside above the village. "So you are going on," said Nicu. "In two days." Nicu rose, giving a hitch to his belt. There was a frown on his face as he looked down on the pattern of roofs.

"I am glad."

I laughed. "Why?"

"Because it would not be good for one of us to stay and the other to leave. I have to go too. My house must be finished before the winter comes. Have you felt how cold are the nights now?"

I had, but unwillingly.

"Can you not stay until Crăciun[1]?"

"No, I shall be in England then."

"If you could come back to the village we should have such fun. It is gay at Crăciun."

"Why do you call it that? "I asked. "The word means more than the day when Jesus was born, does it not?"

"Surely. When the Holy Mother looked for a place to rest she came to the house of a man named Crăciun. He would not let her go into the house, so she went into the stable. That is why we called the day Crăciun."

Nicu sat down again and began to tell me of the fun at Christmas.

"The boys go all round the village to every house singing. They carry a large star. It is made of paper and has a light inside so that you can see the pictures that we paint on it of all the things that happened when Jesus was born. We sing too. Sometimes we act a play. Do you sing at Crăciun?"

I told him that we did, but that I had never seen the star.

"Do you know this song? It is my favourite:

> Listen, John, have you seen
> Or have you heard
> Of my son
> Who is Lord of Heaven and earth. . . .

---

[1] Pronounced Crechoon

131

"But that sounds very like the song that the girls sing of Calojan when you want water for the corn."

Nicu looked puzzled. I watched him, anxious to see if the significance had ever occurred to him.

"Why do you think that?" he asked.

"It is the same idea, a mother looking for her son."

"Of course, yes." Nicu became suddenly excited. "And then later on the song says that the Holy Mother asks why her son has let himself be killed, and he answers that it is because it will make the streams run over and the grass green and everything will grow. But I wonder why it is so."

I shook my head. Very likely he had read at school of Aphrodite and Adonis. I do not suppose that he had as deep a faith in the power of pagan invocations for rain as the older people, but he practised them and enjoyed them, probably turned to them as a last resort. What was the good then of telling him the story of the mother-goddess searching always for her son whose death and rebirth brought new life to the earth, and drawing a parallel with Christianity? If my upbringing and the restlessness of civilization had given me a doubting mind that was my look-out, perhaps something to cure. Though the chance was remote, I should have hated it if Nicu or any of his people had because of me begun to question why they believed this or that. I had learned that it was far better to know only that there is a God who sends rain that the crops may grow and the people flourish, that even if there is no rain they will not starve because the earth is rich and fertile. Fertility is the key; specious argument cannot turn it and look into the mysteries. Men cannot make anything that is fertile, so it is for them to revere Him who can.

The next evening, when we were having our last supper together in Paraschiva's house, I told her that some time before winter came I wanted to go into Bessarabia.

"Bessarabia? That is a sad place. I have never been there. But I have a kinsman who went from here many years ago to Tighina on the river Dniester. It was called Bender then because the Russians had taken it. My kinsman is still there, his name is Vladimir Cercel. You must stay with him if you go, he will help you. It is difficult if you do not know any one, Russia is near, just across the river. I have heard many tales-but you will see."

She wrote a short message on a scrap of paper.

"If you give him this he will help you. He is a good man."

About dawn the next day Nicu and I left. For a few miles our ways were the same and we followed a track eastwards over the hills. Descending into a valley we halted at a fork. So far we had not talked much. It was futile to say how much our friendship had meant to both of us, and we were in the mood when that was all we wanted to say.

"That is your way," said Nicu, pointing to the mountains. "I go straight on till I come to the road by the Olt on which we came."

I held out my hand.

"Good-bye, my best of friends."

He put his hands on my shoulders and kissed me on either cheek.

"We shall not forget one another."

"Never."

He went forward to the building of his house that I should not see, I towards the mountains to a new adventure.

I did not feel lonely. Living with people who gathered their strength from the union of their lives with the earth rather than from constant association with one another had made me look too to something stronger than my fellow creatures, to apprehend directly through the senses rather than bother my head with thinking.

I knew nothing about the village to which I was walking except that it was, like the one I had left, one of the oldest in Ardeal, where the people were as pure Dacian as it was possible to be after the passage of time since the Romans called the land Dacia Felix. I was going there partly because Nicu had to return home and partly because I wanted to see more of Ardeal before I went eastward into Moldavia and Bessarabia. Paraschiva had told me to go to Stanescu, the priest.

Presently the track veered from the mountains and turned eastward along a valley. About four o'clock I came to the village and a peasant directed me to the priest's house. Near to the church was a wall some fifteen feet high and in it were tremendous double-doors with a small entrance to one side. As I entered the courtyard the watchdog broke out into furious baying and a woman came out from a shelter. She eyed me curiously, but gave me a friendly smile. No, the Father was not in, but he would be back soon. Was he expecting me? No? That did not matter. I must have something to refresh me while I waited.

The house formed the left side of the yard. The lower part was of stone with doors in it that appeared to lead to a cellar. The upper part was of wood with a long balcony covered by an immense vine. The woman led me up the staircase to the balcony and into a dim, cool room where she left me. Soon she returned with a bowl of coffee topped with a cloud of smântână[1], the rich cream from a bivoliţa.

After a little while I heard a man's voice in the yard. The priest was

---

[1] Pronounced smintinna

already coming up the stairs when I went out on to the balcony. He greeted me warmly, showing strangely little surprise at my presence in his house. He was a strongly built man, tall and handsome. His full beard was grey, his voice quiet and cheerful. He had merry eyes.

"I shall be happy if you will stay with me. Let me show you your room."

The house had three rooms connecting with one another, all had the shutters closed as though they were rarely used. The door from the balcony let into the middle one, the sitting-room where I had waited, on the left was a larger one comfortably furnished and with many photographs. On the right was my bedroom containing a wardrobe, a washstand, and a real bed.

"It is very kind of you," I said. "But where will you sleep?"

"Oh, I do not sleep here. This house is for visitors and my son when he comes to stay. I live in the little place in the yard where we eat. Shall I show you my garden?"

His garden lay beyond the far wall of the yard behind the churchyard. It was filled with everything that was good to eat and masses of dahlias. We walked slowly up and down, basking in the sheltered warmth of the last sunlight, picking the grapes, shaking the nuts from the trees, and talking. I felt as though I had known him for years. When I admired his garden he was delighted.

"I love it. I am always at work in it. When my son comes he helps me. He is clever, a lawyer in Sibiiu. But though he lives in a town he cannot stay away from here for long, and in Sibiiu he has made a garden for himself. There are many gardens in Sibiiu; no one in this country, whoever he is, can live without soil to dig. Sometimes the Prefect comes too, my son and he are great friends. They are jolly and make me laugh. They are such good boys."

Presently he said that he must see if supper was cooking well.

"Domnica, the peasant woman who cooks for me, is very clever, but I have taught her. I love to cook."

The cabin in the yard had two little rooms. In one Stanescu slept and worked, in the other we ate. There was only just space to move, for there were packed in there a dresser, a chest of drawers which was used as the table, and a sheet-iron stove. As we drank our cabbage soup Stanescu told me of his difficulties in getting the cooking to his taste.

"This, now. It is delicious." He pursed his lips. "But the peasants throw in a cabbage, boil it, and call it soup. I pick only the finest of my cabbages, choose the tender leaves, flavour it with green peppers, put in a little bacon and then. You see . . ." Pressing his forefinger to his thumb he expressed its exquisite delicacy.

So with the fried chick and the cheese pancakes which followed he told me minutely how they should be cooked. It was certainly a meal such as I had not tasted for a long while. The peasants, though they have great quantities of food from which to choose, rarely know how to prepare it. I had always enjoyed the food because I was always hungry and like the full if rather crudely flavoured dishes. But this was a new experience.

I wondered often as the days passed how much time the charming priest spent in caring for his flock. He had been in the village for thirty years and every one loved him. But I believe that above all, save perhaps for his intense love of his country, he was an epicure. He seemed to be always about the yard, looking at his pigs, patting the fat sides of his bivoliţa, working in his garden, or talking with Domnica in her shelter where she cooked.

One day his winter's supply of wine arrived, and we spent the morning tasting from the casks and fumigating the old barrels with phosphorus. The must, the new wine, had to be carefully tested, for it had all to be drunk within two months owing to its continuous fermentation. I did not care much for it. But the matured wine was the most delicious I have ever tasted. Like all country wines those of Ardeal can be quaffed. It is for the men of towns to sit and sip at liquor which has been preserved in bottles. They have not laboured with their bodies, wine means nothing to them but the satisfaction to a cultivated palate. Their palates are like sensitized films, over-exposed they turn black and muddy. Such appreciation is intellectual not physical. But to quaff is to feel the wine run in your veins till you bubble over with the strength it gives you, till you sing and dance. For this wine of Ardeal was not crude and rough, and though it stirred your blood it was not heady. With the glass at your lips the bouquet was of sun-warmed grapes mingled with the smell of earth after rain. I have never drunk so much wine as I did in Ardeal, yet though often I drank late I was as fresh the next day as though I had drunk only water.

I soon learned wherein lay Stanescu's value as a priest. He had never ceased to be a man, and as such had a clear understanding of his people. Though he visited the peasants they more often came to him with their troubles, which pleased him, because he did not like to leave his garden. Leaning on my spade I would listen to the advice he gave them. His quiet voice had a firm dignity, and though he was constantly laughing and joking that dignity never left him. One day as I was entering the yard I bumped into a peasant who was hurrying out, an angry look on his face. Stanescu was standing by his cabin stroking his beard.

"Crainic looks upset," I said. "What has happened?"

The priest smiled.

"He is in trouble with his neighbour. They have quarrelled about the boundary of their land. I have told him that it is no good coming to me alone. If they both come I can help them."

"Will they listen to you?"

"I am their father."

I spent that afternoon carrying sack after sack of corncobs into the loft of the house. There had been a curăţat a few days before I had arrived and the heaped cobs were still in the barn. Domnica's little daughter helped me to fill the sacks; her father, Ion, was out with the plough in the priest's fields.

As the days passed I felt less and less inclined for action. The peace of the late autumn imposed itself upon me as upon the earth and the peasants. The hours became less measured, drifting one into the other. Footsteps were slow, voices long-sounding. There was no wind. All the sheep but those belonging to the village had left the mountains and gone down into the plains. The village flocks were on the lower slopes within easy reach. One could almost hear in the still air the year's breathing becoming deeper and more sustained as it settled to its sleep. Yet, though it was November, the sky was cloudless.

"It will come," said the priest. "Suddenly, when we are not expecting it, the winter will be here. It is always like that. And because the summer has been long the winter will be hard."

Each evening after our supper we stayed in the little room with our wine and cigarettes, talking. As the nights grew ever colder we lit the stove and the warmth and crackling of the wood drew us closer. Sometime Domnica would come and join in the conversation.

"It is good for us to have you here," Stanescu would say. "In the winter my son does not come so much. I have then only the foolish Domnica, her husband, and their prattling child."

"O-ho, so your Domnica is foolish, is she? She will leave you, Father, if that is so. What would you do then?"

"Get one who would not talk so much and cook better."

With a toss of her head and swirled skirts Domnica would leave the room.

When I had been there a week Stanescu received a letter from the Prefect.

"He had hoped to come to-day in time for the wedding. But he is busy and cannot be here till the evening. He asks if you will wait for him, then you can go to the feast together."

"I shall like that," I said.

"Good ! Then we must have a fine dinner ready tomorrow; for to-night you will be late and so will be hungry the next day."

In the late afternoon I was on the balcony cleaning my boots ready for the party when I heard Stanescu calling for me.

"Come here and you will see what we shall eat to-morrow."

He was standing by the door that led into the garden admiring his handiwork. Having killed a piglet, he had cleaned it and nailed it to the door. I looked down and, though feeling a little sorry for the piglet I had seen running in the yard that morning, agreed that it was a fine job.

"Yes, but come closer and I will show you how I did it."

Suddenly as I walked across the yard, an agonizing pain shot through my left thigh as the watchdog, a huge mongrel, set his septic teeth into my flesh. There was no sound; he just shot out of his kennel like an arrow and caught me. But it lasted only a moment. With a shout the priest dashed at the beast and thrashed it off.

"Quick, Domnica, make an iron hot, red hot. We must burn the wound."

But bad as was the pain the thought of being branded was worse.

"No, not that. I have some iodine in my rucksack."

He was back with it in a moment and soaked my leg.

"Burning is better. But I think you will be all right. The dog is always chained and his food is clean."

I was just winding on a bandage when the Prefect arrived. His gay smile vanished in consternation.

"The beast, four tooth-marks. Iodine is no good." He ran back to his car and returned with a tin of petrol. "Now, are you ready? I am going to wash it with this."

I fully expected him to suggest putting a match to it as well. At the end he stood back and laughed.

"What a story you can tell ! You will never lose those marks. You were wandering in a forest and were attacked by wolves. After a brave fight you escaped. Do not forget !"

Domnica's excited face appeared in the doorway.

"You should kill the dog, Father. If it goes mad he will die."

At the fear in her voice I burst out laughing.

"That is right," said Stanescu, "do not take any notice of her, she is full of stupid superstitions. It was not the dog's fault."

"No," I agreed, "it was mine. I thought he was used to me. But he must have thought I was going to steal your meat."

The good old man looked very relieved.

"Go away, you foolish woman, you and your nonsense, and make us some coffee."

Domnica retired muttering and shaking her head.

"No matter how many years after, if it goes mad he . . ."

Stanescu slammed the door after her.

When the Prefect had refreshed himself and I had rested my leg we set out for the wedding party. It was dark by then and the stars shone frostily.

"You will soon forget your leg when we get there," said the Prefect as I limped stiffly along.

"Do you go to many of the peasant weddings?" I asked.

"Nearly all of them. The people like me to go and I love them. When I am there I forget that I am a busy man who has to live in a town. I think then that I am a peasant, and that my life is simple. But it makes me fat. There are so many feastings, births, weddings, funerals. When I am at home I eat only vegetables. My wife laughs at me, but she likes me to go because she knows that it makes me happy and good-tempered. I wish now that you had gone first to the wedding. Here they have still the custom learned from the Romans. When the man goes to fetch his bride she is locked in her house guarded by girls. The bridegroom shouts ' I have come.' ' Why? ' ask the girls. ' For a flower.' ' What flower? ' ' The loveliest flower in the garden.' Then the girls lead out the bride and the man carries her away. They have that custom too in the Apuseni."

The feast was in full swing when we arrived. It was in the bridegroom's house. The room was small and lowceilinged, two long tables were placed in an L along two of the walls, leaving a space for dancing. Outside the door the musicians were fiddling their hardest. First we went straight to the bride and bridegroom to congratulate them, then all round the tables shaking hands and drinking healths. Room was made for us against the wall, our plates were piled high and our glasses filled.

Soon we were all laughing and singing together, eating and drinking without pause. The Prefect was one with them, there was no hint that he was different from the rest.

"I am so happy," he said once, turning to me. "How lovely these people are. It is good to be a peasant."

As the food vanished the țigani threw themselves into a furious tune, and there began a dance of amazing intricacy and speed. It was danced by trios of one man and two girls. They started by whirling in a circle, arms round each other's waists, then, breaking suddenly apart, the man with his hands above his head held the forefinger of each of his partners while they pirouetted around him, faster, faster, faster till their full, white skirts were high about their waists, showing their black-embroidered petticoats. Then at a shout that the crockery on the tables was in danger they came together again, now stepping this way now that, surging together till their breasts and stomachs touched. Away again in a wild swirling till the music ceased triumphantly. Wiping the sweat from their faces they returned to their seats.

Then gently, slowly, picking up the last note of the dance the music sighed into a sad doina, the lament of Ardeal. Love and labour and patience were in it mingled with the streams and the silence of autumn. Joy crept into it with the spring, the fields peppered with fresh green, the sheep going to the summer pasture. The music became faster, the earth was bursting with fruit, up, up it soared and away again went the dancers.

"What is it?" I cried excitedly.

"The Invârtita Haţiegana. It was once long ago the dance of Haţieg[1] near Deva, now it is the dance of all Ardeal."

Jumping to my feet, I seized the Prefect's arm

"Your leg !" he laughed.

"It is forgotten."

Each taking two girls by the waist we whirled on to the floor. It was much too complicated for me, but I felt inspired. A dozen times I nearly fell, but the strong arms of the peasant girls saved me. Round, round, with my hands held high, they swirled about me. Then together, bodies pressing, then away again, their feet twinkling like ballet dancers', mine stumbling. At last, with my head in a maze, it was over.

The Prefect put his arm around my shoulder.

"Why do you not stay with us? We could go to all the dances together. Then you will never forget them when you return to England."

We drank thirstily and leaned back against the wall. I felt wonderfully relaxed; the music had drawn something out of me that had long been wanting to express itself. It had sought me out. As the chatter and laughter was renewed and the music swelled again into slow lament the Prefect turned to me, smiling into his refilled glass, his head cocked a little as he listened to the tune.

"Listen. That reminds me always of a day during the war. I was an officer in the Austrian Army and was then on the Russian front. It was winter and terribly cold. As I walked down the trench I heard the sound of a pipe coming from a dugout. It was long since I had heard such music and I stood listening. I knew that if I went down into the dugout I should have to tell the men to stop playing Romanian music. I could not bear to do that. But I looked and they did not see me. They were squatting on the

[1] Pronounced Hatsyeg

floor listening to the pipe. They were happy, they had forgotten the war and the blood, they were thinking themselves on the hills of Ardeal. Listen !" He began to tap with his foot and swing his head.

> I long and I thirst
> For the leaves of the green wood,
> Our mother the spring
> Blows the dew off the window. . . . "

Soon after I was moved to the Italian front with many others. It was not good for the Romanians to be so near to their country." Laughing, he slapped me on the back. "That is all over. Let us dance."

At midnight we rose to leave. But they would not let us. We were pushed back into our seats and supper was brought in—minced meat rolled in cabbage leaves with chicken broth and peppers poured over it. Then on again with the dancing, surging to a pitch when a fat, old woman, swirling and pirouetting like a girl of twenty, led the Haţiegana with two men. How strong the waists of the girls felt and yet how light they were ! Backwards and forwards, round and round till I was conscious of nothing but a hot beating in me. The Prefect was at the door beckoning; as we neared him I let go and caught his arm, leaving the girls laughing and whirling. Arm in arm we went down the hill.

"How is your leg?" he sang.

"I have none. The Haţiegana has taken them away."

CHAPTER 18

LAMENT FOR CRAINIC

◆

Crainic was dead. The question of the boundary of his land would trouble him no more. He had been in the forest cutting wood for his winter supply. In the pride of his strength he had lifted too heavy a log. Something inside him had twisted. He had managed to climb up on to his *căruţă* and the oxen had drawn him home. His wife came weeping to the priest.

I went then to his house. His eyes had been closed, his powerful body lay with its feet to the open door so that his spirit could walk out, the windows were flung wide. In his right hand that had reaped so many harvests was a coin to pay Charon for ferrying him across the Styx. No knife lay with blade uppermost in the house lest his soul should ride on the blade.

Later, when we stood by his grave, the professional mourners cried and moaned in chorus while the priest read the funeral service. When the coffin had been lowered into the grave the priest blessed the bread which would feed Crainic on his journey. It was put at his head, one big loaf, the *noporogna*, and several small loaves, *colaci*, one for each day of the week to last Crainic until the second *pomană* which would give him further food for his journey.

Then, as the mourners quietened, Crainic's widow broke into lamentation. I wish I could remember all the words of that song. How much of it was extempore, how much thought out beforehand I cannot say. Mingled with her sobs it was yet a song of praise. To my fascinated hearing it sounded like David's lament for Saul and Jonathan.

"How beautiful he was, how strong . . . strong as a sapling which bends but does not break. He could plough in one day what other men could not plough in ten, his arms were like the legs of the oxen which drew the plough . . . his sickle swept the corn down like the wind, like the mountains was his strength as he carried the corn into the barns . . . when he sang the children came to hear him, his love for them was great . . . weep then for him who in the winter once fought the wolves alone that the sheep might not perish, with his two hands he tore them so that those that did not die fled from him. Yet he was gentle as a young girl, as the birds that sing in the willows by the river, even as the ewes was he patient . . . yet he is taken and I who loved him am left, great was his love for me, all his life he was faithful . . . as the sun and the rain love the earth that it shall be fruitful so did his loins give me children. . . . In the midst of his strength he was struck down as the king of the forest by the lightning . . . weep that your tears may wet the earth as the little streams which make the fields green in spring . . . weep for the finest of all men . . ."

And, taking up her song, the mourners wept.

Then the men, with care that their shadows should not fall across the grave and be buried and they die too soon, began to cover the coffin with earth. But before the grave was filled, the widow cried out again:

"O Death, begin your work of corruption at his back, then his legs, then his chest ! O Death, leave his face until the last for it was beautiful !"

The procession left the churchyard. But I did not follow. I had no wish to go to the pomană to eat coliva for the soul of Crainic, such coliva as the Romans had baked of corn and nuts and honey. This pomană would be a desolate feast, tearful, shadowed by death. The ease of short memory which helps the living would not have begun as it would at the third pomană six weeks hence, as it had done at the pomană in the Old Kingdom. Crainic had only started on his journey.

The wailing drifted to me faintly and ceased. Leaning against the wall I heard the switch-switch of Domnica in the priest's yard giving the bivoliţa her evening milking. I stayed there recalling the lament, the age-long paean of the dead's greatness. I had known little of Crainic but that he was an honest peasant, neither better nor worse than any of his people. Yet he had gone to the Shades with a song that moved the imagination like the rhythm of the centuries. Presently the little door of the courtyard creaked open and the geese were driven home honking, urged on by Domnica's shrill cries.

As I moved to go I saw that near me was a grave with a little fir-tree at its head, and looking about I saw that there were several of them in the churchyard. Wondering if they had any significance, I thought, "the fir-tree is the symbol of love, they carry it at their weddings." Then I remembered that the priest had told me that if a young man or girl has died before they were old enough to be married a fir-tree was planted on the grave. He or she had fallen in love with Death.

But Crainic had been struck down in the height of his strength and his fruitful loins, "as the king of the forest by the lightning."

"How are the might fallen in the midst of the battle ! O Jonathan, thou wert slain in the high places."

CHAPTER 19

"IF WE ONLY HAD HAD THE SPADES"

◆

O ne day the sky, which early had been clear, began to cloud over. The clouds dropped lower till no blue remained. The mountains disappeared in the mist and a grey pall hung over the earth. In the afternoon the snow came, and when at night I crossed the yard to my bed the ground was white and the snow still falling.

In the morning the sun shone brightly.

"There will be no snow to-day," said the priest. "We will go to Cisnedoara. I think my son is coming so we will wait for him. How is your leg?"

"All right. Only a little stiff."

The dancing immediately after I had been bitten had not helped my leg. But it was healing well, though ever since I had given it no rest.

"Even so I think it is too far for you to walk. We will go in the *căruţă*. Ion can drive us."

Gavrila, Stanescu's son, arrived at midday and at once every one began to bustle. He radiated energy. Like the Prefect he was clean-shaven and sturdily built, though a little taller. Hardly had he shaken my hand than he was off to look at the pigs, then back to tease Domnica and slap Ion on the back. He disappeared into the garden, but returned in a few minutes to tell his father how fine everything looked. When Ion came up to tell him of the sick calf, he pulled out of his bag a bottle of lotion he had bought in Sibiiu and was soon whispering to the animal, searching for the trouble.

At our meal he talked unceasingly, laughing and joking. He winked at me.

"You have come to the right place !"

The priest had certainly celebrated his son's arrival in his best style. Goose soup, fried chicken, roast turkey, and apple tart. As we drank our wine I said that it was a good thing we were going in the *căruţă*. Gavrila patted his stomach.

"My father gave me this when I was young. If I lived here . . . no, I could not live here, I should die of overeating."

"No Romanian ever died of over-eating." The priest chuckled. "Everything is good for the stomach. Anton, the Prefect—"

"Oh, he has said that to ease his conscience ever since we were at school together."

"Who would think this foolish boy was a lawyer, one of the best in Sibiiu? He never ceases to laugh. I do not know why any one has anything to do with him." Stanescu smiled proudly.

Gavrila's success must have lain in his personality. Though he behaved like a schoolboy on holiday, bursting with high spirits, there was nothing foolish about him. His eyes, like all his people's, had a gay light in them and were quickly responsive to shades of thought, but they were also shrewd and penetrating. His repartee was swift. He did not look his forty years though his hair was grey by his ears. His hands were strong and well-cared for.

The *căruţă* had straw in it to keep our feet warm, and a board laid across it for Stanescu and me to sit on. Gavrila insisted on driving, so Ion sat by him telling him all the news of the village. The springless cart was much harder on my leg than walking, and I was glad when we reached Cisnedoara. It was a Saxon village and looked very neat and prim after the careless, straggling villages I had lived in, but it seemed to lack their warmth of feeling. It was built at the foot of a high, wooded hill. After walking through the village we climbed to the summit where there was a ruined castle built long ago as a look-out and bulwark against the Tartars.

On that cold, still afternoon with winter in the air I felt that I was on a watch-tower looking into the past. To the north the hills and valleys were spread before me, their green fading to grey in the distance. The snow had soon melted in the valleys, but, to the south the Carpathians, white to their lower slopes, lay in a magnificent sweep, barring the way.

The priest looked down on the village.

"This is where I stayed the first night when I fled from my home in the war. At first our soldiers had driven the Magyars before them, but then the Germans came and pushed us back. As the fighting returned towards the village I waited till nearly all the peasants had gone, and then I left too with my wife. Gavrila had gone earlier to join the army in the Old Kingdom. I remember standing on this hill that night watching the flashing of the guns. It looked as though all our precious Ardeal was filled with fire."

"Did you bring anything away with you?"

"What I could. We loaded a horse with my vestments and books and clothes for my wife and walked out of the village." He turned and pointed to a gap between two peaks in the long range. "That is where we crossed the mountains. The Olt valley was crowded with soldiers and refugees. The pass, though difficult, was better. We went on into Oltenia and stayed in Râmnicu Vâlcea. We even took a house there thinking that the Germans could not get so far. But very soon we had to move again, and that time lost all our belongings. We were in Bucharest when the Germans entered the city. They came in triumph. I had joined the army as a priest and was in a hospital when the procession passed. I shall never forget that. The men in the beds could hear the bands playing, and strong though they were they lay crying like children. They could say only one thing: ' We had not the spades. If only we had had the spades they would not have taken our land.' I tried to comfort them. It was terrible."

That was their word, spades. It embraced for them tanks, aeroplanes, steel helmets, gas, machine-guns, all the weapons they lacked possessed by the invaders. In their simple, earthy vocabulary those peasants had no word for these things. The weapon they knew, the one they had wielded all their lives, was a spade. "If only we had had the spades ! "More than a symbol, a cry bursting from the very depths of their being.

"Then I escaped to the army in Moldavia," continued the priest. "I remember seeing Queen Maria there, though there was typhus she went into all the hospitals, talking to the men trying to make them happy. They called her ' our mother.' That is what the peasants call her now. But it was too hard for my wife. The cold and the disease were terrible. She died."

"Yes," said Gavrila. But the sad look quickly left his face. "Mărăşeşti ! We were both there. My father as priest and I as an officer. That was a battle, eh, father? How we fought ! Our army was better then, for the foolish young officers with their paint and corsets who had let the peasants be killed had been disgraced. We fought without them." His eyes gleamed. "That battle lasted for weeks. The Russians ran away because they were Bolshevik, I saw a regiment of them march off with the band playing. We cheered them and laughed, and they thought we were praising them. They could not see a joke. Once I was bathing in the river with the men of my regiment, for it was July and very hot. Suddenly the Germans made an attack. We had just time to get our knives. We fought naked and drove them back. But though the Germans could not beat us at Mărăşeşti we had to make peace. The promises of our allies were empty. We should all have been killed in the end. And what is the good of the earth if you are dead?"

"What happened after that?" I asked.

"I could not yet return to my village," said Stanescu. "So I went to Russia. Many of our people have lived for a long time in the south of Russia, even as far as Odessa."

"Did you hear of what our Government did?" broke in Gavrila, laughing. "When the Germans came near to Bucharest it sent all the crown jewels and all the money in the banks to Moscow for safety ! We trusted the Russians then. Millions and millions of lei all gone. No wonder we have no money !"

"I was in Russia for two years. The Russians had not killed God then in the south." Stanescu crossed himself. "The priest in Elisavetgrad had died so I looked after his parish. The richness of the church was wonderful. Everything was made of gold. Then the Bolsheviks came. They arrested me and sentenced me to death. But I escaped. When I returned to my village everything was gone. There were not even doors nor windows—nothing. But soon the peasants helped me, Gavrila came back and we were all happy again. We have never hated any one. No peasants in any country hate those of others. It is governments and men who do not suffer who make wars, and then we have to fight or our earth would be taken from us."

"My holy father is being serious," laughed Gavrila. "You must not be serious about war. Though they are wicked fools who make it, they are still fools. Laugh and forget it. Brrr ! I am cold. Let us go home."

So we jolted back through the falling darkness, through a forest where the priest said the wolves would be coming soon now that winter was near. Domnica welcomed us with a roaring stove and table spread. Our stomachs warmed, the priest told us of his childhood, of old folk-lore and strange superstitions, and Gavrila capped them with tales of were-wolves and vampires while the night pressed icily against the windows.

Though the succeeding days became bright and warm again the signal for my departure had been given. The snow had come. If I was to reach Bessarabia before winter set in I must leave. I was sorry, I loved the old priest and we had become close friends. Each day we looked at the sky and told each other that autumn was not really over.

One morning as I lay on a hillside in the warm sun I heard a piping near to me. I could not see the player, he was over the shoulder of the hill with his sheep. It was as though a passing wind had found a reed on which to sing of its wanderings, mimicking the sigh of the forests, the splash of streams, drawing its notes long as it crossed the plains, rising tirelessly over the hills, syncopating the nod of the flowers. There was strangely little of man's music in it, only the stressing of certain phrases made me aware that a man was making it, taking the earth's music as he heard it and dwelling on those parts of it which affected his senses or his memory deeply. For an hour or more I listened. The shepherd paused rarely, and then only for a few moments. As I went down the hill I passed below him, he was seated among his sheep his staff by his side, and did not look up from his playing.

I had descended to a side of the village where I had not been before, and on the outskirts came to a house with a richly carved doorway leading to its yard. An old peasant was seated on a log outside whittling a stick. I had never seen him before but asked him if I could take a photograph. The door was old and the carving on it unusual. To my surprise he was nervous and hesitating. He was not sure if I could; he would go to ask his wife. I heard them discussing the question in the yard, and, after a few minutes, they both came out, followed by the family. The woman shook her head and protested strongly. No, I certainly could not take a photograph of them. I said politely that I need not take one of them, I wished only to take the door. But it was no good. She took her husband by the arm and hurried him and her family back into the yard, shutting the door firmly.

I felt wretched. It was like suddenly being slapped in the face by a friend. True, I did not know them, but I had become so used to being kindly treated that I could not understand it. I began to wonder if, after all, I had been an intruder only people up to now had been too polite to tell me so.

But the priest laughed away my fears when I told him.

"It is a superstition. Many of the peasants still believe that evil will come to them if their photographs are taken. They think that it draws their spirits out of them and that they will die. They have many ideas like that. You remember at the funeral of Crainic the men who dug the grave did not let their shadows fall in it. A man cannot live without his shadow, they say. If a house is being built there are many who will not walk by it if the sun throws their shadow on it lest it should be walled up and taken from them."

On my last day in the village, Anton, the Prefect, and Gavrila came to fetch me. The Prefect had asked me to spend the night with him in Sibiiu. They came early, for Gavrila wanted to prepare a piece of the garden for a plantation of fruit-trees which would later be planted in his garden in Sibiiu. We divided up the work, each of us taking a portion to trench and manure.

By six o'clock the light was almost gone and I had completed my rows. I stood aside, leaning on my spade, while the others sowed them. Gradually there crept over me a sense of unreality, a feeling that I was dreaming in my bed at home and soon I should wake up to see my familiar room with Henrietta there, and hear my child gurgling somewhere near. The voices of my companions sounded indistinct and jumbled as though I was listening from far away. Beyond, through the open doors of the shed where the sick calf was lying, I could see the fire in the yard glowing in the darkness. A cauldron hung over it, and the steam from the soup rose in clouds coloured by the fire. In the shadows stood the bivoliţa, its head looking grotesque as the flickering light played on it. Domnica was milking her, switch-switch, switch-switch in a steady, drugging rhythm.

I think it was then I realized for the first time how strange was the world I had been living in. Yet, though it was different from anything I had ever known, I had drifted into it without knowing where I had crossed the border-line of new experience. It was as though I had been carried through time to be shown a state where simplicity of life produced the strength and beauty which restless complication and progress had lost. But there seemed to have been no break in the continuity of my life since I had left England.

Our farewells were protracted, every one's health was drunk, Domnica's, Ion's, and their little girl's included. So the sadness of our parting was mellowed. Kissing the old priest on both cheeks I climbed into the car.

"Do not forget us," they cried as we drove out of the yard.

It was late when we came to Sibiiu, but Anton's wife was waiting up for us. She was a Saxon, tall, slim and unusually dark, with a small head, fine, steady eyes, and the classic features of a Greek statue. I have rarely met so gracious or beautiful a woman.

As my time was now growing short I had decided to return by train to Bucharest and find my way thence to Bessarabia. Before going to bed Anton and his wife gave me much good advice as to how I should proceed. In the morning Anton came to my room and made me a present of the embroidered night-shirt he had lent me.

"It will make you dream of us," he said. "Here are two other things as well to keep out the cold."

He handed me a painted, wooden bottle, a plosca, filled with ţuica, and an immense, brown căciulă[1].

"I bought that căciulă in Bessarabia; take it back with you. It is very thick and will keep you warm."

He came with me to the station. As I was saying goodbye to him and the train was about to leave, a tall, bearded figure appeared on the platform, glanced around and hurried towards us. It was Stanescu.

"I could not let you go without seeing you again," he panted. "Now I have almost missed you. We started early, but one of the horses cast a shoe. Ion is here too. He has brought a present from Domnica for your wife."

He beckoned to Ion, who came forward and gave me a beautifully embroidered blouse rolled up in a newspaper.

The train grunted, stopped, and then lurched on its way. The waving figures disappeared. I was alone again on a noisy, swift thing that I had almost forgotten. The hills of Ardeal gave place to the mountains of the south. Braşov, Câmpina, Sinaia with its summer palace of the king. . . .

[1] Pronounced kerchooler.　A round, high, sheepskin cap.

Ardeal was gone.

> Oh, poor, strange land
> How long have I kept watch with you?

They will sing that still, though they are happy. They will sing it, though it is sad, for the beauty of its sadness.

CHAPTER 20

THE JOURNEY EASTWARD

◆

In Bucharest I found a man who was going north to Bucovina by road and he agreed to give me a lift. I had not wanted to hurry through Moldavia, feeling that that part of the country, though I should only get a superficial view of it, would prepare me a little for Bessarabia.

Leaving Bucharest in the evening it was dark before we came to Ploeşti[1] where we were to spend the first night. The dull glow which had hung before us in the sky became deep red as we drew nearer, and away to the right of the road a great furnace shot its flames high. I thought an oil well or a refinery had caught fire. But my companion laughed.

"It is fuel oil. Millions and millions of litres have been burning for months. It cannot be sold, there is no market for it. They have bought expensive machinery to help in the burning of it. Even that is cheaper than trying to store it, it is useless."

Oxymoron!

Ploeşti was a cosmopolitan and dirty town, the centre of the oil district where Germans, English, Americans and Romanians had their offices and refineries. It reminded me of a large, western American town that had sprung up over night and looked ready to fall down again as quickly. The only bright colour in it was the market filled with peasants who had come into the town with their produce, and even they looked dirty and depressed. The smell of oil hung over everything.

But the wind of the corn plains of Moldavia soon blew me clean again. Hour after hour we drove over their interminable expanse. To the west the heel of the Carpathians sank below the sky line, to the east the earth curved away till it was lost in a purple haze. In the late afternoon we stopped to change a tyre. The stillness was absolute. The earth, naked of its crop, was asleep.

We passed through no villages, they lay away from the highway across the plains. The collections of houses flatteringly called towns were small and poor, there was too little reason for their existence for them to be otherwise. Perhaps they had been villages once but the highway had given

---

[1] Pronounced Ploesht.

them other ideas and spoiled them. We slept that night at Focşani, a dismal place.

The next day the land became more undulating, and in a short time we came to Mărăşeşti. On a little hill stood the memorial to the battle. In summer the sea of corn swept up to its doors, now only the furrowed earth billowed to the horizon. The building was circular and low-domed. In the centre was an altar enclosed in a small room. Off the corridor which encircled it were thirteen rooms, about ten feet long and four wide, each with a window looking over the plains. In the walls were recesses built in the shape of coffins standing on end, the stone lids stood askew revealing shelves on which were rows of broken skulls. In one room stood a flag leaning by the window, a cold breeze blew through the iron grille rustling the dry crown of bay leaves with a sound like the whispering of spirits. There was a smell of death. I was glad to leave it. Beyond we crossed the river where Gavrila and his men had been caught bathing and had fought naked with their knives.

Towards evening we climbed a long, wooded hill and from the summit saw Iaşi, the last sunlight making its roofs and windows bright against the dark, surrounding earth. We turned off down a narrow lane through the woods till we came to a village, beyond was the house of the boyar, Pavel.

The barking of his dogs brought him to the door. He was tall and walked with a stoop, his long, narrow head thrust forward. His hair was grey and his face lined with the weather and his age.

"I am so glad you have come," he said to my companion in a measured voice. "It is long since I have seen you. And you have brought a friend, a friend brings good luck."

I was surprised at the smallness of his house. It was built on one floor, like a peasant's, with a veranda in front. But it had six rooms furnished in good taste, Romanian, Russian, and Turkish rugs covering the divans and the floor. The furniture was mostly peasant-made, some of it finely carved. Old maps of the countries of Europe hung on the walls, the ceilings were low and beamed.

When we had finished our supper we lay on the divans while Pavel talked.

"You have come to know our peasants," he said to me, "and you like them? "

"Yes."

"You are right. Though as a landowner I have suffered, I like them no less. Perhaps you wonder why I live in this small house. It was once my overseer's. As you know, before the war, there was more corn grown in this country and Ukraine than anywhere in Europe. But though that meant money it was a bad affair. Money is not everything. The peasants had little land, it was nearly all owned by boyars and many of them spent their time abroad in Paris and other places. They left their land to overseers who were often bad men. The peasants did not have a good time. They never have. It is they who have always struggled for the country. When Kutuzov came to Moldavia he said he would leave them only their eyes to weep with. But that was long ago."

"They are patient," I said.

"Yes, indeed. But they sometimes revolted. It was in 1913 that they burnt my house. There was a great deal of unrest in that year. But it hurt me that they turned against me." Pavel shrugged his shoulders. "I had always cared for my land and my people. The peasants may be the life-blood of this country but a boyar is not close to them. They did not hate me, I think they liked me. But they had been upset. It was really absurd." He laughed at the recollection. "I was here when they came. Though they were excited they did not try to hurt me or my family. They were almost polite. They just would not let me try to save anything while they burned all I had. Afterwards they were sorry. But what was the good of that?"

"What happened afterwards? Did they continue to work for you?"

"Of course. But I had no house, so I lived here. I had started to build again when the war came. When the war was over I returned. My overseer had been killed, so I continued to live in his house. I have not so much land now and cannot afford a bigger one."

"Did the Government take away a great deal of your land?" I asked.

"I have only five hundred hectares now. It was hard. But I do not feel angry about it. So long as I have horses to ride and enough money to live in comfort I do not care. I have always lived simply. Why should the peasants not have the land? For hundreds of years they have worked it like serfs. Is it strange that I, a landowner, talk like this?"

I could not help smiling, and acknowledged that it was. He nodded and raised a finger at me.

"You see, my friend, in this country we do not all care for money. What we like is peace and to be let to do as we like so that we can enjoy ourselves. When the peasants worked for us we did not worry about them because we had all we wanted. But many of us thought that it was unjust. More and more of us thought this till at last, after the war, the Government, as you know, was strong enough to divide the land among the peasants. In the Old Kingdom, Banat and Ardeal the old landowners were left with five hundred hectares, in Bucovina two hundred and fifty, in Bessarabia one hundred. We were promised compensation." He spread out his hands. "The lei lost its old value. It is almost nothing."

"I wonder that the landowners have not fought against it."

Pavel made a grimace which lifted his eyebrows and turned down the corners of his mouth.

"*Laissez-faire, laissez-faire*. Neither we nor the peasants are savages under a thin skin, half-Asiatic, like the Russians. We are gentle, perhaps too gentle. To us, however born, it is the earth that is important. Those who made money out of it only wasted it, it was no use to them. So now that they see that their chance to make it is gone they . . ."

"*Laissent-faire*" I finished for him.

Pavel rose and stretched his long arms.

"Exactly, and every one is happy. There is no money, the Government is at its wits' end because no one will lend it any, other countries say we are hopeless, but no one here can starve."

"What about the towns?"

"The towns?" He snapped his fingers. "If men want to live in towns they deserve to starve. But here they do not. Food costs almost nothing. Listen. If a man has land and no money he does not want. If he has money and no land he will always want, because however much he has he will want more things than he can buy. One lei or a million it is all the same. ' The earth satisfies, money desires.' You have heard that? Well, we are happy, what matter?" He yawned. "Forgive me, I am tired. I wish I was your age. Shall we go to bed? You will be starting early in the morning."

Pavel roused us at six and we soon came to Iaşi[1]. There was no time to spare if we were to get to Cernăuţi[2] by nightfall as the road was bad, so I saw little of the university town. It had many fine buildings and was a clean, thriving place with a feeling of warmth and homeliness.

"It has more students than Munich," said my companion. "It is full of ideas," he added a little scornfully.

As we entered Bucovina the country changed. It became very hilly, almost mountainous in parts, and around us were the great beech forests which give the country its name. The sense of approaching winter here was less acute. The trees gave shelter from the keen wind. In the hollows there were still flowers in the village gardens. I saw that the peasants' clothes were not so gay as in the Old Kingdom, the colours of the embroidery were deeper, more subdued. Towards evening we passed women returning from the fields, some carrying their babies on their backs, strapped to a board.

What I saw of Cernăuţi was so like an Austrian town that it seemed almost strange to hear Romanian spoken around me. This was not

---

[1] Formerly Jassy.   [2] Pronounced Chernauts.

surprising, as in 1775 the Turks who had dominated Bucovina had handed it over the heads of the Romanians to Austria in thanks for her checking Russia's ambitions in Moldavia. From then, until 1918, when Bucovina declared for reunion with the Old Kingdom, it had been a part of Austria, its capital Cernăuţi or Czernowitz as it was then called.

But it did not interest me to stay, I wanted to be with the peasants again. In the morning I left my companion and took a train south-eastward to Kishineff.

At first there seemed no noticeable difference in the country from that which I had seen before. The forested hills of Bucovina dropped behind me and we came to plains like those of Moldavia. Then gradually I felt that the land was broadening out, long, low hills swelled nearer, the valleys between were wide. It was like emerging from a land-locked sea into an ocean. A distant tree-top showing alone above a hill appeared as the mast of a ship hidden in the trough of a wave.

I became impatient and restless, the journey seemed endless. At last in the afternoon I reached Kishineff. I had about an hour to wait there for the train to Tighina on the Russian frontier and so walked into the town. I was taken by surprise. For in plan Kishineff is Russian, Bessarabia having been a part of Russia for over a hundred years until it was reunited with Romania after the war. From its population, a hundred and sixteen thousand, I expected an imposing city, but it was more like a vast, overgrown village with a main street so long and straight that, from its centre, it vanished to a point at their end. It was bitterly cold, the wind sweeping through it as though it was a channel between the Poles. I drew my *cojoc* tighter around me and pulled Anton's *căciulă* over my ears.

There is something melancholy about an almost empty train, it seems to have so little purpose, and there were so few people about that I wondered if I had got into the wrong one for Tighina. I had a compartment to myself, and taking the *ţuica* out of my rucksack took a long and warming drink. Then settling myself into a corner I waited for the land to unfold itself.

The sun was low, a red, wintry ball when we started. The train was a small, black worm in the immensity of the steppes. It followed the contours of the earth, curving and climbing and running down inclines like a child trying to prevent itself from falling. Now and again we came to wayside halts, a collection of huts dwarfed to the size of toys by their surroundings. When we stopped a mantle of silence fell, shouts sounded loud and clipped, losing themselves, dissipated in space as soon as they were uttered. The sun went down in a stormy sky, the wind, which had

ceased for a while, rose again, harshly whistling around the carriage
windows. To the east the earth rolled without end. Somewhere near was
the Dniester, for I knew we ran parallel to it for some way, but I could not
see it. It was somewhere in the trough of a wave. Beyond it was Russia,
now hidden in the gloom of approaching night.

Though the journey was not long I became very cold; more țuica to
warm me made me sleepy. At a halt the voices in the next compartment
rose and fell droningly, making me close my eyes. I was awakened by a
voice, and looking up saw a tall, old man peering at me with bleary eyes.
He was shouting,

"Is every one dead? I am lost. Where are we? Holy Mother, no one
cares for a poor, old man."

"Nor a young one," I replied. "I do not know where we are."

"But we are at a station."

I might have suggested that in that case he could easily find out. But he
looked so ancient and forlorn that I jumped up and went outside. We were
at Tighina.

"Thank you, thank you,"he wheezed. "Is my son there?"

I looked up and down the deserted, little platform, and then back at
him. Again I felt prevailed on to help him. Talking down my rucksack I set
off.

"Do not leave me," he shouted. "Help me down. I am so old."

He shambled along beside me to the waiting-room. When he saw his
son there he left me and opened his arms to him, kissing his bearded face.
They went out together into the night.

There was no one else in the room but the man behind the counter,
who was smiling at me.

"He is a queer one. Once a year he comes and it is always the same.
He is always lost."

I felt lost too. So I ordered some vodka and asked his advice. Drawing
out the piece of paper on which Paraschiva had written I showed it to him.

"Vladimir Cercel. No, I do not know him."

I tried to help his memory.

"He does not live in the town but a little way outside in the country,
near the river. He has a farm."

The man scratched his head.

"Vladimir Cercel—Cercel. Ah, yes, of course, he comes here sometimes,
a short, square man with a big moustache."

I said may be, but I did not know.

"It is a long way, you cannot walk. If there is a carriage here you will have to take that. Will you not eat first?"

It was already about eight o'clock. Vladimir was not expecting me, knew nothing of me. What if he had no room for me, though I banked on his natural hospitality for that. All the same I was a stranger butting in out of the night. The oil lamps in the waiting-room stank suffocateingly, the air, though warm, was clammy and fœtid. I said I would go.

The man obligingly came with me to find a carriage and give directions. Outside the wind blew through me like a splinter of ice. In the road was a droshky, its driver sitting like a mummy, muffled to the eyes in his long gown.

We rattled through the long, straight streets of the town. There were not many people about and the dim-lit streets looked lonely. The lamps grew farther apart, and ceased. The houses straggled away till only a few stood at intervals by the roadside. The night was black. There were no stars. I could barely see the hunched shape of the driver before me. But for the bumping and lurching of the droshky I might have thought myself in wind-filled space.

"Is it far?" I shouted.

But the reply was blown away from me. The wind curled about me, whipping at me as though it wished to lift me from my seat and plunge me wailing into the surrounding emptiness. After about half an hour the driver turned off the road towards a light. By a house he stopped, but did not move from his seat. So I climbed out and rapped on the door.

"Vladimir Cercel?" I asked as a man appeared framed in light.

"Yes. What do you want?"

Anxiously I fumbled for Paraschiva's note, and as he read it apologized sincerely for coming upon him unannounced and at night. He rubbed his face, looking amused.

"That is all right. Paraschiva ! Well, well ! Come in."

I told him there was a driver outside, so he shouted to him to enter.

"It is cold. We must give him a drink."

He led the way into a little room and soon we were all warming ourselves while he politely asked me all the questions he could think of. The driver, now that I saw him in the light, was a huge man, only his eyes and nose showed through his whiskers which ended in a long beard. He became very merry and was singing when he drove away.

"Now, let us go to bed," said Vladimir. "We will talk in the morning. My wife is not here, my children have grown up and flown. There is room for you and I am glad you have come."

I was tired and fell asleep at once. I do not know how long I had slept when a sound awoke me. The wind had dropped a little and now soughed gently around the house.

Rat-a-tat ! Rat-a-tat-a-tat-a-tat !

With the sound breaking on my newly awakened consciousness I stared into the blackness above my head trying to focus my mind. I was still in a half-dream and with a fancy of the past stirring in me thought of an angry rattlesnake I had once met. In the silence and the darkness it made me tingle uncomfortably as I strained my ears, waiting for the sound to come again. A single report broke the tension. It seemed to come from far away as though in answer to the query that my mind had raised.

As I turned myself on my elbow, the vicious patter snapped out again, fixing my determination to find its cause. I groped my way to the door and out to the room where Vladimir was sleeping. His door was ajar and at my knock he stirred.

"Eh, eh, what is that?" he grumbled, striking a match.

"That sound?" I said. "Listen !"

"Eh, it is nothing." He laughed throatily. "It is only the Bolsheviks. They do that every night to frighten people. You will soon get used to it. Let me sleep."

The match flickered out and I returned to my bed.

CHAPTER 21

ONE MORE RIVER TO CROSS

◆

T he world looked naked when I went out of the house next morning. It was as though the gale had swept away its last covering, baring its body to frosts that would bite deeply, to the snow that would come presently to warm its ice-cracked skin. Every detail of the vast landscape was clearly defined, even to the farthest hills which lay darkly under the hurrying clouds. Where the blue of the sky showed it was pale, washed out, changing its shape continuously as the jagged strips of grey torn from the slowermoving masses of cloud were swept across it.

From the yard I could see the track where I had left the road the previous night, and beyond, sometimes hidden by folds in the earth, sometimes rising and running straight for some distance, was the road. I could trace its course to the outskirts of the town. Vladimir's house was on the edge of the village, which was like any village in the Old Kingdom but that the roofs were mostly thatched with reeds. The air resounded with the morning excitement of geese released from their pens, pigs ran snuffling in every directions, while the geese pecked at the piglets' tails. Vladimir came out to me.

"So you did not sleep well?"

"I woke once," I admitted half-ashamedly.

He laughed and patted me on the back.

"I thought you would know about the noise. It is nearly always like that. If the wind had not been so strong you would have heard it before you went to bed."

"But what was happening?"

"I told you. All the time there are Russians trying to swim across the river and escape into this country. If the Bolshevik soldiers see them they shoot at once."

"Surely they were not killing people last night?"

He shrugged his shoulders.

"Perhaps. But I think not. They let off guns at night to frighten the people so that they will not jump into the water. Of course if some one does go into the water they kill him if they can. They have lights too which they send up to shine on the river. I am used to the sound; I hardly notice it."

I nodded with a feeling of horror mingled with amazement at Vladimir's apparent disregard.

"I should like to see the river some day," I said.

"Of course, why not? Sometimes there are fishermen on it. It is not far." He pointed to a belt of low-lying forest to the east of the village." Over there. How long will you stay?"

"I do not know," I answered vaguely. My anxiety as to the time I had left seemed to have been taken from me. I felt dwarfed by immeasurable distance.

"To-morrow I go to the market in Tighina with the last of my best apples. Will you help me sort and pack them to-day?"

I agreed gladly. I wanted to get my hands to work with something again. It would help me to become used to my surroundings.

So all day we worked in the yard, sometimes peasants came in, talked, helped a little, and went away. The fruit had long been picked and was stored in a barn. Tenderly we picked over the unbruised apples, laid them in wooden crates, and staggered out with them to the *căruţă*.

"I have a fine orchard, but the fruit this year has not been good. For three years the crop has been bad. It has been the same all over Bessarabia. The country is terribly poor." He stood back munching an apple. "It is the same with the corn and the vines. The wine here is the finest in the country. Before the war it used to go to St. Petersburg, the Czar was very fond of it. But now for years we have had either floods or no rain at all, or else there have been late frosts. Everything has been spoiled. The people do not know what to do. This year there has been no rain for the corn and the frost took the apple-blossom."

The blustery afternoon darkened early, and as we went into the house grey sheets of rain swept across from the west. Vladimir went out again to catch a chicken while I made up a roaring fire. Later when we had eaten and were sitting by the stove one of the men who had helped us for a while with the apples came in. He stood in the doorway shaking the water from his *căciulă*.

"Brrr ! What a rain ! I have been at the *cârciumă*[1] and could scarcely see my way. The wind took of a piece of Stascu's thatch the other day. He was lazy and now the water is coming in."

He laughed and at a nod from Vladimir helped himself from the bottle on the table.

---

[1] Inn. Pronounced kerchumer

"Noroc !" he said, raising his glass.

"We are going into Tighina to-morrow, Josif. I have wondered what domnul Englez could do there. I shall be busy all day."

Josif thought a moment. He was younger than Vladimir, clean-shaven, lean, with a high forehead and deep-set eyes.

"I can come too if you like. Then, while you are at the market, I will take him to the Prefect. The Prefect may give him permission to see the fortress."

"Yes, that will be good." Vladimir, chuckling, told him how I had woken him the night before.

Josif nodded. "Yes, it sounds bad if you do not know about it."

I tried to picture the country in my mind's eye. Bessarabia is the long strip of land about sixteen thousand square miles in area running north and south between the rivers Prut and Dniester, ending at the south in the Black Sea and in the north touching Poland. The Dniester is the narrow, twisting boundary.

"Is it very difficult to escape?" I asked. "The frontier is so long. It must be over eight hundred kilometres."

"Difficult ! The Bolsheviks have a soldier about every three hundred metres the whole way, and machine-gun posts as well. That is why we have to have such a big army, we have to guard the river too. The Bolsheviks are very clever. It is not only refugees who come across."

"No, indeed," said Vladimir. "They are always sending their spies over to make trouble with us. Bessarabia is full of them, though we try to keep them out."

"Do the people listen to them?"

"A few. The lazy ones who think that they will live without work if they are Bolsheviks. Just now it is bad because the crops have been poor. The Bolsheviks say if they were here the crops would be good. People do not believe that of course; we know why they are bad, we know the earth too well. The spies think themselves very clever. But people are upset; it is natural. One year of good harvests and all that would be gone. If we were starving there would be trouble, but we cannot. Over there," he jerked his thumb, "they do starve, and we know it."

"It is funny sometimes," laughed Josif. "Do you remember the story I told you about when I stayed with my kinsman in Ciopleni near Kishineff?" He turned to me. "There was a Bolshevik who had come to that village. When he told every one all the fine things that communism would bring the people listened to him. One day there was a crowd with him and he chose an old man from the rest so that he could explain what he meant. '

Now suppose you have two cows,' he said. ' You keep one yourself and give the rest to the community. Do you understand? ' ' Yes, that is excellent,' answered old Naie. ' If you have four horses, you keep two and give two to the community.' ' Yes, that is very good.' ' If you have six pigs, you keep three and give three to the community.' ' That is good too.' ' And if you have eight sheep, you keep four and give four to the community.' Naie shook his head. ' Oh, no, that is not good.' Then the Bolshevik became angry and said he was stupid because he had agreed when he had asked him about the horses, the cows, and the pigs. ' That is so,' said Naie, ' since I have no horses, cows or pigs, but I have many sheep.' It was very funny. Every one laughed and the Bolshevik looked a fool. Most of us know that we could not be given more than we have, and that perhaps the Bolsheviks would only take what we have away from us."

The next morning we trundled off early to the market, joining the procession of căruțe coming in from the country. As we entered the town I saw that it was a smaller edition of Kishineff. Though its population was twenty thousand it had no large buildings. The streets were all straight, very broad and lined with acacias; from the crossroads they stretched away till they were lost in a dip in the ground or swallowed by the distance. I saw no house with more than one storey; the place was like a huge village. Notices were in Russian and Romanian.

The market was in one of the side streets. On either side the căruțe heaped with produce were lined up, the horses, which were mostly shaggy ponies, facing the road. Josif went off on some business of his own, and, after watching Vladimir haggling with the dealers for a time, I went for a walk through the market to keep myself warm. Here and there were braziers, a crowd of men and women round them buying roasted nuts and gossiping. When I returned I found Josif waiting for me. We went together to find the Prefect.

Though he appeared to be very busy, he was willing to help me in any way he could. There is always time for conversation in this country. He wrote out a permit and handed it to me.

"I am sorry that I cannot give you permission to see the fortress," he said. "Only the Ministry of War can give that. You see, we have to be very careful here. But if you take this with you you will be able to go down to the river near to it. Also you can see some Russian refugees who have swum the river; they are here in the town. Afterwards when I am less busy please come back and we can talk."

Where the fortress stood the bank of the river rose steep and high so that it overlooked the surrounding country on both sides of the river. Josif and I walked down to the river's edge and showed our permit to the sentry. The stream was not so broad as the Thames at Westminster. Half across it stretched the bridge that had once joined the two countries. Now from the Russian side it came only half-way, the Romanian half was buried in the river, a jumble of twisted iron, a piece of railway line sticking out from the water. The Bolsheviks had blown it up in 1918. On the far bank a soldier paced up and down clad in a grey great-coat and a flat hat. He pointed across the river to us and shouted something to the men behind him, his voice sounding clearly.

"It's all right," said the sentry to us, laughing. "We don't want to cross. They need not worry."

Josif looked at the river. "Soon it will be frozen. It is terrible then. The people try to cross over here on the ice. The Bolsheviks shoot them down, men, women, and children. But sometimes the men kill the guards. Last winter in this district alone about a thousand escaped. It cannot be so pleasant over there. Have you seen enough? Let us return to the town."

As we walked back Josif asked me if I would like to see some of the refugees. So we went to the building where they were housed. There were fifteen of them in a miserable room about twenty feet by twelve in size with one small window. The guard called them out in to the yard and told me I could talk with them. In face of such dumb misery I felt suddenly ashamed at my inquisitiveness. If I had been there to do something for them I might have felt better, but I was like a man visiting a zoo. I wished I had not come. The men were of all ages, thin almost to emaciation; their faces had a transparent yellowness and their eyes were ringed with pink. They looked wretched and spiritless. Racking my brains for some question I asked them why they had escaped. Their stories were mainly alike. The wages paid by the Soviets bore no relation to the price of food. They preferred to risk death quickly in the water to slow starvation. One of the younger men said that his parents had been bourgeois, and that he had never been given a chance to earn a living. Another stood a little apart; he was middle-aged and took no notice of what was going on. He just looked at the ground without moving, his face blank and hopeless. I felt that I could not approach him. But the guard saw my glance.

"He has been like that all the time. His wife was drowned."

It was too horrible. I could not help it, what was the good of my staying? I wanted to lose those faces. Outside I told Josif I would like to see if the Prefect was free.

"It is better in the afternoon," he said. "Let us go back to Vladimir and eat."

Vladimir had sold his apples. So we sat in his cart eating bread and cheese and later went to have a drink. About three o'clock I found the Prefect, and we talked for an hour or more. I asked him about the wretched condition of the refugees I had seen and what would be done with them. He shook his head.

"It is very hard for us. All the time there are these people coming over. We have to arrest them at once, because we do not know who are refugees and who are communist agents. If we cannot discover what a man is we have to send him back. I do not know what happens to the poor devil. But we cannot help it. The rest we spread all over the country. They settle on the land, work well, and become happy, I think."

"It must increase the population a great deal."

"Yes, indeed. There must be about a hundred thousand in different parts of Romania. But we cannot turn them away while we have plenty of land and they do not plot against the State."

"But how do you tell whether they are refugees or not?"

"At first we were often deceived. Now we can tell better. A great many of them have kinsmen in Bessarabia. Until after the war Bessarabia had been a part of Russia for a hundred years, so they used to move backwards and forwards. Besides, on the other side of the river in the Ukraine and nearly to Odessa, there is a large population, about a quarter of a million, which is Romanian. If you were to go there you would see that their language, their customs, even their dress is the same as ours here. The Soviets, knowing this, made a Moldavian Soviet Republic over there, and gave the people more freedom, because they hoped that those here would think what a fine place it was. A lot of peasants believed them at first. But now the Soviet has become as cruel there as everywhere else. So every one is trying to come back and many, many Russians as well. It is very hard for us to know what to do with them."

I asked him if many went the other way attracted by the prospects held out by communist agents.

"Yes, a few. Our position is this. Bessarabia is mixed. Nearly three-quarters of the population is Romanian, but there are also Bulgarians, Tartars, Germans, Russians, and even a colony of French Swiss. When the Russians ruled us their idea was to make us Russian and their method was to keep us ignorant. The zemstvos ruled for the Russian boyars who could not see the end of their noses, they spent all the money on great buildings, hospitals, and so on, which were never used because there was no more money. The peasants were not considered, they were almost serfs. Well, when the revolution came the country was in a terrible state; everywhere were wild bands of Russian soldiers, drinking, murdering, raping. Then for some months we broke away from Russia and had a Moldavian Republic here. But it was no good, the Soviet beyond the river were too strong; they sent over troops and soon we were in danger of becoming a part of Russia again. So in 1918 we decided to become reunited with Romania, which is what every one but the Russians had always wanted. Gradually the country became peaceful. We do not wish to quarrel with Russia, we should like to be friendly. But for some years there was bad trouble with the communists, though now it is better."

"If it were not for the bad harvests?"

"Ah, yes. You are staying with the peasants. But is it the towns which suffer, though there are not many in Bessarabia, and those who live in them. Most of the townspeople are Russians and Jews, because the Russians kept Romanians out of business when they were here. The peasants are nearly all Romanians. You ask if many cross into Russia? As I said the people even in the towns have been kept ignorant. Some look around and say, ' Look at the bad harvests, the poverty of the land; the communists invite us, over there it is perhaps better.' But the peasants, no. They may be ignorant of books but they are very intelligent. They see the people escaping in thousands from Russia and they say, ' What kind of place can that be that so many want to leave? It must be a very bad one'." The Prefect laughed and rose from his chair. "No, my friend, we can look after ourselves. Continue to live with your friends the peasants. They may grumble, but they do not lie and they can see straight."

Indeed I was happy to return to Vladimir and Josif, whom I found waiting patiently in the road with the căruță. I had had enough of politics. That night around the fire we talked of Paraschiva, of Ardeal, and told each other stories. Sometimes we sang.

CHAPTER 22

NIGHT OVER RUSSIA

◆

The wind, after a short respite, returned with venomous fury, clawing at the thatches, the hayricks, the fences, everything it could grapple with its icy fingers. The fowl, swept off their feet, sheltered miserably in the barns. The cattle stamped and complained in their stalls. Away by the river the forest bowed and moaned, while now and again there was a crack as a rotten trunk resisted the eddying blasts no longer and fell sprawling, its arms caught in the surrounding branches. Few people were abroad and the fields were empty, crouching desolate under the rearing flail. Across the sky the clouds raced and twisted like the vapour from an immense cauldron.

The second day of the great gale we went out to find Vladimir's slatted fence lurching about the yard like a tethered snake. We spent the morning mending and strengthening it. In the afternoon we drove in the *căruţă* to Tighina to fetch his wife, Marina.

"See whom I have with me," he said as she stepped down from the train. "An Englishman."

Marina was muffled in a great, black shawl, so I could see little but her smile.

"And so that is all you have to say to me," she cried. "Nothing of what a terrible journey I have had, nor that you are pleased to see me. ' See whom I have with me'," she mimicked, hurrying down the platform. "And the wind around the train so that I thought a thousand wolves were after me. What a husband ! Men are all alike."

Climbing in the *căruţă*, she huddled herself in the straw while we piled in her parcels. Now and then as we were buffeted along the highway her voice would scream out a piece of news.

"Vladimir ! Do you know Moise's wife is going to have a child, she is like-" The rest was clipped and swept away from us.

"What?" bellowed Vladimir over his shoulder. Then, to me, "Moise is our eldest son."

Presently she knelt up, her head by our elbows as we sat on the driving-seat.

"Vladimir ! Have you mended my loom yet?"

"Yes. Lie down, woman, you will be frozen."

Marina subsided into the straw, only to rise again with some fresh question or gossip.

It was exhilarating driving over the swept earth, the wind singing and howling about us and Marina, excited at returning home, fighting constantly for breath. At length the horse was stabled and we went into the house. Marina, panting, threw off her shawl. I saw then that she was about fifty, a little woman, tough and wiry, with a round face much weathered, and keen, bright eyes.

"Ah, it is good to be home again. Not for six years have I left this house, long before Moise was married. Now I can welcome you. Have you been well? Has Vladimir looked after you?"

She shot the questions at me, chuckling.

"Perfectly," I replied.

"Good, good." She turned to her husband. "Wake up the fire, man; we must have food."

Vladimir set to work, grumbling good-naturedly.

"She is full of herself, and thinks she can order me about just because she has been away for a month. In a few days it will be different."

But Marina was not listening. She bustled in and out of the room, moving furniture, disappearing, returning, and chattering the whole time.

"So Moise is going to have a son," said Vladimir as we sat down to table.

"Oh, so you have remembered. But you do not know it will be a son."

"We always have sons."

"Maybe. But you cannot have children with women. More than that, Moise has four cows. Think of it ! We have only two."

"Has he an orchard, though?"

"You and your orchard that never bears fruit ! No, he has not an orchard. But you should see the corn he has had this year. As for his wife, though I never thought much of her, she works hard. Yes, indeed, she has been in the fields with him all the autumn, without her he could never have got in his harvest, and do you know that . . ."

On, on she went, pouring out all her news like a river in spate, while Vladimir listened patiently, now and then interjecting a remark. I did not speak at all, though she smiled at me continually so that I should not feel that I was left out of the conversation.

In the morning Marina's excitement had quietened, and though at times it erupted she was busy all the time about the house. Later we fetched her loom from the outhouse where it had lain all the summer and set it up for her in the living room.

"Now," she said, "I must work. There is no more to be done outdoors, and our clothes have worn out."

After that she set herself to preparing her threads. The long winter had started, the time for work in the house, when the women wove their clothes and those of their menfolk. They forgot the storm outside. The earth needed their labour no longer, it was sleeping, waiting for the snow to come, to cover it, to pass away and leave it black and rich with slender spikes of green thrusting upwards from the new birth. Then they would go out again into the fields, on Sundays they would wear the gay embroidery they had made on those short days and long nights; there would be dancing and weddings. In the week the sweat would dry on them under the fierce sun as they moved slowly over the earth. Midsummer, rain they would pray for, harvest, curățat, and then the autumn would shine and fade, the winds would come and again they would be, as now, in their houses. Round, for ever would go the cycle of their lives and of the earth.

What stories I heard too in the evenings, as, leaving her loom, Marina worked flower patterns on the blouse she had spread over her knee. She had started on the blouse towards the end of the previous winter, but she had not had time to finish it when the spring had come.

"On such a night as this there are vampires," she said, as wisps of straw from the yard driven by the wind tapped at the window.

"What are vampires?" I asked.

"There are none," laughed Vladimir.

"Indeed there are. You can tell them by their pale lips, and nothing can save you from them but a cross held before them. You cannot kill them until they are dead. Then you can stop their evil on earth by driving a stake through their hearts."

"Nonsense, woman !"

"You say that because you are afraid. Do you not remember Grigorie, the miller at Husani? No one knew why he was rich, he was always cheating the people, but they could never prove anything against him, he was too clever. They did not dare to say he was a vampire, but they believed it. After he had died they opened his grave, and when they put the stake through his heart the blood spurted out red."

"That is long ago. There are none now."

Marina snorted. "So long as there are people on the earth there will be vampires."

"Why?"

"Because there will always be some who dry up the souls of those they live with."

One day Vladimir took me to the monastery of Noilui-Neamţ[1] at Chiţcani[2], a village some seven miles away near the river. Every time we climbed a long hill I looked expectantly for a new view, but every time it was the same, another long valley, another long hill, endlessly rolling country. Did it ever end, I wondered? From the summit of the monastery's bell-tower I looked far over into Russia; there was no change in the scene. Was it like this all over there, across Siberia, China, till the waves of the earth dissolved in the waves of the Pacific? It seemed as though it must be.

Vladimir told me that the monastery was immensely rich, one of the richest in the country. The vineyards produced the finest wines, the orchard the finest apples. A high wall surrounded it, and within the walls were three churches. The Bolsheviks had shelled it several times, there were jagged rents in the bell-tower. A shell had fallen right through the roof of one of the churches, narrowly missing the shrine of the Virgin Mary. The roof had been mended and the shrine decorated with tinsel and flowers to commemorate its miraculous escape. The abbot insisted on my taking its photograph.

It was with difficulty that we escaped his invitation to spend the night. He pressed us anxiously, showing us the guest-room and plying us with food and wine. But we would not stay. Any moment the snow might come, and when it came it would fall heavily. So with a bottle of his golden wine and his blessing we walked homeward, our heads bent to the wind.

I awoke in the night aware of something having happened. Uneasily I wondered what it could be. Then I knew. The night was still, the silence deathlike.

In the morning a weight seemed to have fallen on the earth. All life seemed to move with leaden feet. The lowing of cattle was continuous and melancholy, the cackling of geese was like spirits crying out in terror at their doom. The trees were motionless as stiffened corpses, stretching their black arms against the sky. Great ravens, driven by the storm to hide in the woods, returned in flocks, hovering above the houses in search of food, settling darkly on the frozen fields. The sky was livid, hanging low, as though with the sudden ceasing of the wind it had fallen closer to the earth, ready to blot it out. To the north huge masses of purplish-black clouds mounted steadily, folding and unfolding with slow, terrifying motion like an octopus sucking its way over a rock. The light was feeble, struggling to be day. Over all hung a dull silence.

---

[1] Pronounced Noolwe Nyamts.   [2] Pronounced Kitskan

"It is the snow," they said. "It is coming now. After it will be brighter."

But my midday only a little had fallen, the earth was hardly powdered by it. I watched anxiously, for at night Vladimir and I were going down to the river. I had said I had wanted to see the Russian town of Tiraspol by night. He had shrugged his shoulders and said that there was no real risk. We had the pass which we could show to the guards. I had decided to leave the next morning, so we were going up the river bank from Tighina. It was unwise, he said, to go straight through the forest from the village to the river as we might get lost in the darkness, and anyway it would not do to come suddenly on the guards by an unfrequented track.

In the afternoon the air cleared a little, though it was still heavy. Rents appeared in the gloomy canopy, revealing patches of blue sky, pale like the reflection of icebergs. The light was cold. As night came on the moon showed itself at intervals, at first wanly then brighter, frostily, as darkness fell.

We ate our supper early and set out. I said good-bye to Marina. I should not see her again as I was going to sleep in Tighina, and take a train about dawn. Then it was as always: "La revedere," the hope for another meeting. "I am sorry I was not here at first," Marina said. "But I am glad you came. It has been good fun for all of us." Her keen eyes brightened. "How glad you will be to return to your wife. It is not good to be away too long. I know."

For some time after she had lost sight of us, her figure stood in the lighted doorway looking into the night. Then the door closed and I had left another home.

In Tighina we put the cǎruţǎ in the yard of a friend of Vladimir's and set off towards the river. Soon the town was behind us and we entered the belt of swampy forest that stretched away down the river bank. The night was clearer now, still and icebound; by the light of the moon, which now and then disappeared behind clouds, we wound our way along the narrow track, parting the tall grasses that tried everywhere to conceal its existence. Every now and then a sentry loomed up, calling us to halt. I showed my pass and we went on. There was a tenseness in these marshy woods which made me wonder why I had come, what I hoped to see that would satisfy the curiosity that had brought me there.

Before us, around many bends in the river, a glow hung in the sky above Tiraspol. After walking for over two hours we drew near to it. We could not as yet see the town when the sound of motor-horns came to us shrilly across the water. I halted. Standing there with the high reeds and grasses at my shoulder, the forest still, with no sign that there was any life on earth beside mine and Vladimir's, I thought I had never heard anything so strange as that sound striding the night. The river seemed to separate two worlds and the horns were as the present mocking the centuries with empty laughter.

Abreast of the town was a clearing with the guard-house and soldiers. The opposite bank was brilliantly lit. Square factories, their windows shining, towered above the lower buildings. In a square, open to the river, motor-cars crossed and recrossed. I could see few people, yet there was a feeling of intense, mechanical activity behind it all. I remarked on it. One of the soldiers laughed.

"Those lights. Oh, they mean nothing. They shine all night whether any one is working or not. They are only to make us feel what a poor place this is and what a bright, busy town is Tiraspol. Men who have crossed have told us that nothing of any worth comes out of those buildings. All the towns on the river are like that. The Bolsheviks hope that we shall think that they are gay and prosperous. Besides, with all those lights, it is hard for any one to escape from the town."

I asked him if it was dangerous work guarding the river. Sometimes it was, he said. A few nights before when he had been on guard beyond the town he had caught a man and a woman just as they came out of the river. He had brought them up to the officer of the guard, who in turn had put them in charge of a soldier to conduct them to another post farther down the river. Midway between the posts the Russian had turned quickly on his guard, grabbed his rifle, and driven the bayonet through his body. Then leaving the dying man on the ground, the man and the woman had jumped into the river and swum back to Russia. I asked for some explanation of apparently so pointless an action. The soldier shrugged his shoulders.

"It was along the path you have come. Those people are strange. Their minds are not like ours; we do not understand them. Nicolaie had done no harm, yet he died the next day. He was only a boy, doing his service like me. Perhaps the man was a spy—but what good did he do? Only, God knows, we are near to death," he ended, crossing himself.

It was late when we started on our homeward journey. Tiraspol was quiet. But its lights would shine all night, illuminating the river. It was some eight miles to Tighina with never a break in the gloomy woods. We had gone over half-way when, after the usual challenge, Vladimir stopped to talk with a sentry he knew.

I left them and, going on a little way, drew my *cojoc* around me and sat down on a hummock by the bank to rest. Gradually the brooding horror of the place caught me. But for lonely shots the night was absolutely silent. The intense cold laid itself against my face, numbing it. Across the river a sentry strolled slowly, the moonlight bringing at times a quick glitter to his bayonet. There came to me then an awful sense of my powerlessness conveyed by that land of endless steppes, a land which folds and unfolds itself for ever. Across Bessarabia, over the river beyond that man, across all southern Russia, on, on. . . . I felt too that in such a vast land one human life more or less could be of no importance to any one, that the immensity of the country must swallow up the meaning of individuality. Only in such a place could human beings continue to die for no other reason than that they wished to seek happiness on one side of a river that they could not find on the other. Even the man who shot them had maybe no clear idea why he did it. Perhaps he thought that there were so many miserable human beings that the loss of a few could make no difference. More likely he did not think at all. With a black weight on me I wondered indeed if it did make any difference.

At the house of Vladimir's friend, where I was to sleep for a few hours, we parted.

"It is strange that we have met," said Vladimir. "But I am glad. Next time you come we shall have had good harvests, every one will be prosperous, for the earth never fails."

It was still dark when I caught the morning train. Then the sun came over the rim, ponderous and dull with streaks of bloody red, lighting the steppes with an almost transparent clarity, the swampy lakes reflecting the brilliance in their morning-grey waters. But soon, so rapidly that only half-watching it I did not see it pass, the colour was gone. At first thinly and lightly, then more heavily till the sky filled and the earth was hidden, came the snow.

EPILOGUE

◆

I t was already dusk when, on a lonely country road a few miles outside
Bucharest, I arrived at the gates of the castle. A peasant came out of the
lodge to open them, and I passed down an avenue where the naked
branches high above my head formed a dark network against the sky. In
the hall the livery-servant told me that the princess had give me up and
had gone for a walk in the park. She would be back soon and had left a
message for me to wait.

He led the way up a broad staircase to a long, pillared and low-vaulted
room, where he left me. On one side were arched windows, wrought iron
gates outside them, facing on to a balcony. Through its colonnade I could
see a lake. For a time I sat by the crackling fire while the quiet of the
seventeenth-century room grew around me. I was reminded of a Venetian
palace; there was in there that same mingling of the West with the East.
Presently I walked up and down the gold mosaic floor looking at the books
which lined the walls, at the silver silk thread of the chairs, and at the
woods beyond the lake.

I did not notice the princess's entrance. Her long black and white gown
moved with the shadows in the room.

"I am so glad you have come," she said. "We have a lot to talk about."

I apologized for my lateness, the car in which I had come had broken
down.

She laughed. "They always do. We are not very good with machines
here."

Sitting by the fire we began almost at once to talk about the peasants.

I had come here with a purpose. I had had to spend a few days in
Bucharest before returning home, and in that interval I had become rather
unhappy. The town seemed to have so little in common with the country
of which it was the capital. The atmosphere too was filled with the foul
chatter of the foreign press which had sunk to its periodic and ignorant
abuse of the country's ruler. True the Romanians took little notice,
shrugging their shoulders at such deplorable lack of taste. But those English

who had long been there were angry and ashamed, and I with them. They knew the truth about the country and its ruler's struggles which outsiders made no attempt to understand.

So, on this my last night, I had left the city, gone back to the country to find the link that would bind together all that I had felt and seen, to gather together the present with the past, the peasant with the noble, and find an integrity that would make me happy again.

Listening to the princess I became content. As she spoke of her people, I recalled the days I had spent in the villages; the walls of the castle opened out to admit the countryside, the plum orchards, the fields of tasselled maize, the little hills and the willows by the streams. The room was peopled with peasants and the panorama of their earthy life.

When she had been married to the prince whose dynasty went back six hundred years to the great Basarab she had been little more than a girl. She had always loved the peasants and had spent a great deal of time with them, so that as she had grown older they had known her not only as a princess but as one of themselves.

"' They are dirty and lazy and immoral.' That is how those talk who do not know them," she said angrily. "But those are words that have a town meaning, a wrong meaning. Their dirt is earthy, their laziness is the intelligence of men who do not hanker after money but work only enough to provide for themselves and their families. You know how hard their work is. If they had not time for careless enjoyment when would they dance and sing their songs? And are they not beautiful? Immoral indeed! A girl must have a good wedding. Sometimes a man has to wait for years before he can give her a wedding of which she shall never be ashamed. Does it matter if their love cannot wait till then to give them a child?"

She told me then about her husband's grandfather. In his days the țigani were slaves. He had had three hundred of them, they had lived around the castle, making glass for the windows, furniture for the rooms, every article that is now bought in a shop. When in 1846 they were freed, the țigani had to be turned out. They were miserable, they had nowhere to go. So he had built them a village, it was called Ţigăsneşti[1]. I had passed through it on my way. There were many such all over the country.

We covered the whole land in our talk. She knew it intimately, lovingly, and told me so many things of which I was ignorant that my desire to set out again was quickened. Of the Lipovans who live on the mouths of the Danube, among whom the patriarchal system still prevails, and where, when the son of the house is to be married, the father often takes the girl into his house for a year before she is given to his son. The centuries fell

---

[1]Pronounced Tsigeneshty.

away to the flocks of Abraham.

As I was leaving she took me into a great, scarlet bedroom, fit for the lying in state of a cardinal. There was a painting there of a sultan ordering the beheading of a Basarab, with all his sons.

"The sultan wanted to destroy my husband's line. It was a peasant woman who saved it. She had been all her life in the Basarab's service and substituted her son for the baby of the family. A peasant can proudly say in this country, ' Sunt Român'. Because of her I am a princess !"

The next day as the train took me away over the Moldavian plains a falling wall of white covered my sight as it mantled the earth. I was content. The cycle of seasons would turn there now without me. From harvest to harvest life would run in a perfectly composed circle, the earth its centre, the core of its existence. For a time I had been within its compass; I did not want to look in from without. "The spades, if only we had the spades."

It was dark long before I reached the Polish border. I was tired of reading, and closing my eyes listened to the pounding rhythm of the train. The sound called up the rhythm of the songs and the dances till it blended into a steady stream as I fell asleep, a steady and powerful river of labour and song like the giant artery of the land:

> On the banks of the Danube
> Go the youths with oxen.
> Before the oxen
> Go with lovely flowers
> The finest of the young men.
> The sun cries to the flowers,
> " Go, dear flowers, more swiftly
> For the great Danube is coming. . . ."

If you enjoyed this book then try another title from Bene Factum Publishing.

TRADITIONAL FRANCE…CLASSIC WRITING…

TWO VAGABONDS IN LANGUEDOC
Portrait of a French village
By Jan & Cora Gordon

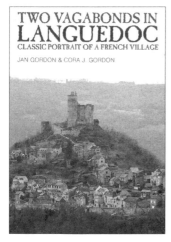

Imagine a village in deepest rural France, where life is unhurried and old-fashioned courtesy and gentle banter prevail – you need look no further than Najac, a sleepy medieval village overlooking the languid Aveyron River in the Department of Tarn.

It was here in the early 1920s that two very eccentric English artists, Jan and Cora Gordon, arrived one summer's day intending to spend the night…they left four months later. The result? *Two Vagabonds in the Languedoc*, one of the greatest and most endearing travel books ever written about France.

This book is 60 years or so pre-Peter Mayle, but it captures France to the same degree for not much changes in those parts. The witty and perspicacious pen-portraits of Najac's inhabitants – the priest, the doctor, the hotel-keeper, the judge, the baker, the blacksmith and a wonderful collection of village and farming characters – together with lively accounts of village life combined to convince the Times Literary Supplement of the day that this was *"one of the most remarkable books we have read on France for a long time…."*

With a highly informative introduction by Ken Bryant, the leading authority on the authors and their official biographer, Bene Factum have produced an

illustrated paperback facsimile edition of the original imprint, which has the great advantage of including the charming sketches made by the Gordons during their stay in Najac.

The return to the bookshelves of *"Two Vagabonds in the Languedoc"* is long overdue and should be one of this summer's most popular books for all those heading for France on holiday and, of course, for those English legions who now live there.

Note on the authors: Jan & Cora Gordon were an exceptionally talented couple who wrote twelve captivating books about their travels between 1916 and 1933. In their day they were something of a publishing phenomenon. Working as artists in Paris Jan & Cora met and married there in 1909. On the outbreak of WWI they joined the Red Cross and found themselves in the Balkans. After the war they returned to Paris and combined their literary and artistic skills to write and illustrate their first travel book about Spain. Success followed success. In the late 1920s their growing international reputations led to a grand tour in the USA and further popular books on art as well as several novels.

Illustrated paperback
Price: £10.99   Pages: 264
ISBN: 978-903071-11-3 (1-903071-11-9)
Published by Bene Factum Publishing
PO Box 58122, PO Box 58122, London SW8 5DZ

WINDS OF SORROW:
travels in and around Transylvania

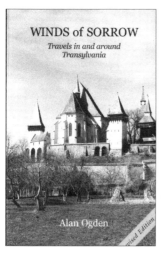

WINDS of SORROW
Travels in and around
Transylvania

Alan Ogden

"Winds of Sorrow" is an eclectic collection of essays compiled by the author during his travels to Transylvania in northern Romania between 1998 and 2004. What was at first a mere inkling of a name on a map in a faraway Ruritanian land unfolds into an exotic medley of fascinating people and picturesque places. The complex truths behind the convoluted history of Transylvania are revealed as the reader journeys to the medieval towns and villages of this former Principality, once famous throughout the courts of Europe. These are journeys not to be missed!

"In this meticulously researched account, Alan Ogden swiftly drives a stake through the heart of the vampire myth....Ogden is an energetic - and eccentric guide- scampering around churches in search of crumbling frescoes..."
The Guardian, 4 December 2004

"Ogden demonstrates with tremendous enthusiasm that, far from being an irrelevant backwater, Transylvania is crucial to a true understanding of Europe.... Winds of Sorrow adds significantly to a body of work that amounts to a valuable contribution to European culture, testifying to the tenacity of its virtues as well as to its horrors."
The Spectator, 20 November 2004

"The rural areas, a microcosm of mediaeval life, are filled with proud and generous inhabitants. Images of smoke, darkness and inclement weather contrast with gorgeous vistas, the luminosity of church art and the beauty of an unsullied countryside."
Geographical magazine, January 2005

Written and Photographed by Alan Ogden
Orchid Press: ISBN 988-97764-1-3